RUSSELL BUDDY HELM

Drumming the Spirit to Life

LET THE GODDESS DANCE

2000
Llewellyn Publications
St. Paul, Minnesota 55164-0383, U.S.A.

FIRST EDITION
First Printing, 2000

Book design and editing by Connie Hill
Cover photo by John Millen, ThunderHeart Drums
Cover design by Anne Marie Garrison
Interior photos by Cathleen Javier, Marcella Zinner, Charles Turkington,
     Lynne Alexander, Teri Smith, Wriston Jones

Let the Goddess Dance, on which this book is based, was originally hand-published at *Seasons,* "the most unusual gift store," 1021-A Montana Avenue, Santa Monica, CA 90403, 310-395-1965. Copyright R. S. Helm 1998. All rights reserved.

Library of Congress Cataloging-in-Publication Data
Helm, Russell Buddy.
     Drumming the spirit to life : let the Goddess dance / Russell Buddy Helm. —
1st ed.
          p.   cm.
     ISBN 1-56718-432-4
          1. Music—Psychological aspects.   2. Drum—Methods.   3. Spiritual life.
     I. Title: Let the Goddess dance. II. Title.

ML3920.H42   2000
786.9'11—dc21   00-021800

Llewellyn Worldwide does not participate in, endorse, or have any authority or responsibility concerning private business transactions between our authors and the public.
     All mail addressed to the author is forwarded but the publisher cannot, unless specifically instructed by the author, give out an address or phone number.

Llewellyn Publications
A Division of Llewellyn Worldwide, Ltd.
P.O. Box 64383, Dept. K432-4
St. Paul, MN 55164-0383, U.S.A.
www.llewellyn.com

 Printed in the United States of America on recycled paper.

Drumming the Spirit to Life

TAP INTO THE RHYTHM OF LIFE

We have not only a responsibility to ourselves to play and feel rhythm, but also a responsibility to the world and the Universe. By freeing ourselves through rhythm we become members of a greater whole—a whole that has been there all the time. Rhythm is life itself. By playing we connect to what is important.

The Universe is waiting for us to play. It needs us to play because the Gods like to dance. As individuals and in groups, we articulate the beat that is life, awakening the life force in all things. A sense of rhythm is a sense of life and rejuvenation that is essential to a well-balanced, integrated, successful partnership with life. And it's fun too—if you're not smiling, you're not doing it right.

ABOUT THE AUTHOR

Russell "Buddy" Helm is a multimedia artist and teacher who started classical music training at the age of eight. As a teenager he developed his skills in various musical styles: rhythm and blues, rock, country, folk, and spiritual. With his band, Bethlehem Asylum, he opened for the original Allman Brothers group, and went on to play with many great blues performers such as Chuck Berry and Bo Diddley. He also played and/or recorded with Frank Zappa, Tim Buckley, Big Joe Turner, Pete Ivers, and many others. In addition to albums, his work appears in soundtracks for films. He also works in television and video production, both with live performance and with computer graphics. He was post-production supervisor for Lorimar on the *Falcon Crest, Knot's Landing, Hunter,* and *Dallas* series. A teacher as well as a performer, he gives individual lessons and workshops on drumming. Also an artist and sculptor, Helm's work is shown at several California galleries, as well as in Atlanta and Philadelphia.

email: buddyrsh@ix.netcom.com **website:** BUDDYHELM.COM

TO WRITE TO THE AUTHOR

If you wish to contact the author or would like more information about this book, please write to the author in care of Llewellyn Worldwide and we will forward your request. Both the author and publisher appreciate hearing from you and learning of your enjoyment of this book and how it has helped you. Llewellyn Worldwide cannot guarantee that every letter written to the author can be answered, but all will be forwarded. Please write to:

Russell Buddy Helm
℅ Llewellyn Worldwide
P.O. Box 64383, Dept. K432-4
St. Paul, MN 55164-0383, U.S.A.

Please enclose a self-addressed stamped envelope for reply, or $1.00 to cover costs. If outside U.S.A., enclose international postal reply coupon.

This book is dedicated to all the people
who don't think that they
have a sense of rhythm.
You do. We all do.

Thank you to Eileen Trafford,
my first drum teacher,
and to Cathy Javier
for her unlimited help and support.

CONTENTS

ACKNOWLEDGMENTS

I want to acknowledgment and express my deep gratitude for all the people who have contributed in any way to this book:

Cathy Javier and Lily, our Great Dane

All the friends of Seasons

Jumoke Anoff-Sylla and Papa Sylla, supplier of great drums and information about Africa

Panji for the Djembe

Shelly Boston, Doctor of Chiropractics

Marcella and Charles Zinner

Winifred and Carl

Lily, Russell, Roy, Chief Many Horns, and Sister Mary Lucretia

Thanks to all the stores, healing centers, and drumming groups across the United States that have sponsored my druming workshops over the last seven years, and to:

Lynne Alexander

Diane and Richard Daffner

Wriston Jones

Steve Sanzo at Bungalow Productions in Eagle Rock for great production on the Drum Dance meditations

Eileen Trafford, a gifted teacher and amazing drummer

All the people who have been drumming through all the years of time

Ron and Laura, Sky Stone Eagle Lambert

XIV   ACKNOWLEDGMENTS

Thanks to Baba Olatunji for showing us the inspiration
 of love in the drums

Thanks to Gregory for explaining the mysteries of sound
recording

Thanks to the musicians who taught me

Thanks to my music partners, both living and dead.
The music is for you

PREFACE

A SAFE SPACE

People have come to me and asked me to teach them how to play drums. I have been playing since I was about eight years old so it is something that I don't think about. It just happens, but I do have to *feel* the rhythm. If the feel is not there, then it is hard work. I have done that kind of drumming too, as a job, but this book addresses the joyful aspects of drumming—the feeling type of drumming rather than the thinking type of drumming. It deals with the spiritual drumming that so many people are hungry to experience. It also deals with courage—the courage to hit the drum, and to keep on hitting it.

Having a safe space in which to discover one's own drummer is important, a space where people can experiment and learn to participate in the group experience. At Seasons we have managed to provide such a space and the result is very rewarding. Healing energy is one of the most profound results of this kind of group drumming. There is a therapeutic and integrating effect for the body and the soul. This safe space doesn't have the concerns about wrong notes or performance anxieties. There isn't any competition in this kind of space—the beat supports everyone. This is the real power of the drum.

I have heard such wonderful healing stories from people who have connected to their sense of rhythm that I am compelled to continue providing this space, even if it is not a physical place but a state of being. Drumming is something that I have always done. It is a constant in my life where other things are not. This realization is a source of strength and confidence for people who are lost in the rush of civilization. Finding one's own drummer is finding an old friend. I encourage women and men to create this safe space for themselves as drummers and dancers. Ultimately one of the main things that this book is about is to create a safe space for the inspired dance that is in all of us. Our culture needs to understand that this dance is sacred and shouldn't be interrupted. First things first though—we must find the rhythms that enable us to dance. This will happen for you if you listen and play and enjoy yourself.

I thank the people who have come to me with a desire to learn to play drums. Their courage in seeking their own safe space in which to learn is commendable. They have drawn the teacher out of me and I have become more of a human in the process. It is the students who create the teacher, and in a real sense it is the student who teaches, because I have learned what I must tell these people by listening to their lives and sharing in their attempts to understand their own rhythms.

In some cases I have merely given permission to the people who needed to hear it from someone else. They then give themselves permission to feel their own sense of power. This power is manifested in the sound of the drum. When they hit a drum and get a good tone, that tone vibrates through their whole bodies and through their whole lives. It is their own drumbeat and they are playing it themselves. That first note is the most important. It is when they finally overcome the fear of their own power, but the second beat is also important because that means that the rhythm will go on. Then each beat after that is also important, because each beat means that the rhythm will continue and that the drummer is alive and part of a continuum.

When we overcome our performance anxiety in life, we can share our own rhythms with the world and the universe. By playing the drum we create a safe space. It is a miraculous phenomenon that I cannot explain. All I know is that it works.

This book is an attempt to translate the drumming energy into words. The drum was invented to articulate the other realms only accessible through the drum. This is a translation from a language without words. There are no definitions in our culture for what is taking place when the drums are being played. Drumming is a creator, a conduit of power. The student who is humble receives that life energy in large quantity. The proud ones only make a lot of noise.

Gye Nyame: I am prepared, I will win, provided God does not decide that I should lose.

(Adinkra proverb)

1
FROM THE
BEGINNING

Drumming has been a part of human life for longer than anyone can imagine. Starting in dark prehistoric times when humans were living a simple existence in the caves and forests of Europe, the savannas of Africa, the cold Arctic, the remote Himalayas, or the sensuous Caribbean, people were playing drums for healing, prayer, and joy.

The drum is a deceptively simple tool for power, healing, and joy. Technique is not that important. What is more essential is the *feel* of the rhythm. Good drummers don't always play a lot of difficult, fast notes. More often, a sparse, simple pattern will create the desired effect. Especially for beginning drummers, the goal is to allow the effects of the steady, repeating beats to filter down into your body, spine, hips, and heart. When this happens there is a sense of well-being and connectedness to nature and life.

When first hitting a drum with your hand, two primarily different tones are available to you. From the center of the drum head comes a deep note: a low, meditative tone that speaks to us in a deep ancient voice that our bodies can recognize on a basic, cellular level. It is an ancient friend calling out to us to join the eternal rhythms of the universe and the dance of life. Then, at the edge of the drumhead is a higher-pitched tone that cuts through the distractions of everyday technological life. It speaks to our minds while the lower voice speaks to our bodies and heart.

Our bodies and minds respond to these voices with relief. We feel safe when these tones vibrate in us. We begin to heal, and we feel a sense of joy.

By quickly slapping the drumhead in the center, eliciting a deep tone, we exert power and force in a controlled, peaceful manner. There is no violence in hitting a drum. It is more a quick light pat that brings the voice up and out of the drum. Hitting the head quickly, getting the hand off the head as fast as possible, so that the skin can vibrate, is the first technical challenge for beginners. This happens when the player can relax his or her wrist, yet maintain a certain amount of muscle tension for control of the hand. Drumming has many graphic analogies of balanced opposites. This first example is rewarding when we achieve a balance of tension and relaxation in the wrists that gives us the right tone.

There are no wrong notes when playing a drum in this way. There are only clues to what can be played next. The inner critic is a busy survival technician, constantly evaluating what the person is doing and judging whether this activity is correct in terms of survival. Playing a drum is not a survival activity; it is a method of release and joy. The inner critic is not really needed. Eventually it will give up its attempt at monitoring every note that is being played and go on a vacation. This is what is desired because only then can we really begin to be the drummer that is in all of us. The most important thing to remember at the beginning is to keep playing the drum. Don't stop in the middle of a rhythm and say, "Wait! I made a mistake!" This is the inner critic struggling to stay in control. The second analogy of opposites in drumming is that we must let go of our inner critic in order to be in control of the rhythm.

The main reason that the inner critic cannot keep up with the inner drummer is that the brain is a cumbersome and awesomely large computer. The brain is programmed for learning. Once the learning process has happened, the brain activities move too slowly to play the fast patterns. The neuron signals flash back and forth between the hands and the wrists too quickly for the brain to be engaged. The brain delegates the activity down into the muscles of the hands, the arms, the wrists, and the feet, where it belongs. Up to this point the drummer may feel a sense of frustration at not being able to get the pattern. This is a good sign. It means that the inner critic is at its optimum level of processing information. It is ready to give up and just let you play. So when the feeling of being dumb or of not having any talent gets almost overwhelming that is when the inner critic is ready to give up. So, take a big deep breath, let go of the frustration, forgive yourself, and, by all means, keep playing.

Trance is a state in which we can talk to God.

We all have a sense of rhythm in our bodies, even those of us who say things like, "I don't have any sense of rhythm," or "My parents never gave me music lessons," or "I'm too uncoordinated to play," or "I'm a girl," or "I'm a man," or "My race doesn't have natural rhythm," or any other silly rationale for avoiding the joy of feeling rhythm in our bodies. Technological cultures sublimate the individual's sense of rhythm into an organized, productive form of expression such as work, religion, sports, or war, but we all have our own personal sense of rhythm beneath the layers of cultural conditioning. The challenge now is for us to reconnect with our own sense of rhythm. It is one of the oldest forms of healing and self-integration.

In some historical situations our sense of rhythm has been categorized as being somehow less than civilized; someone's natural fluid rhythmic movement is labeled socially unacceptable, lascivious, sinful, or pagan. This comes from centuries of getting people organized and focused on maintaining an ever-enlarging social order and increasing productivity—which is fine—but this imperative creates rigidity of thought, action, and philosophy. The results on the individual are physical and psychological stiffness. This subtle need of the human organism for expression of rhythm has not adequately been taken into consideration. What has been misplaced is the individual's secret personal connection to the life force. Moving to and playing rhythm is a natural activity that has always provided this personal cosmic connection to the Divine.

The drum is a power tool, a simple effective way of generating life force in the player as well as in the listener and the dancer. In a sense, the drum is a battery. By playing the drum, the rhythms of life are brought into graphic display for all to appreciate. The greatest musicians, such as jazz players, remark that the music flows through them like a current of energy. When playing a drum, this energy flows through the player and the instrument. In some way, the drum is embued with this energy. The more it is played, the more energy is stored up. The drummer can set the drum down and come back later for a recharge. The energy will eventually dissipate from the drum if it is left to sit on its own, so it is good to remember to pick up your drum and play it whenever you can, in order to keep the energy level alive—in yourself and in the drum.

Another reason that the individual has not been allowed to experience their own sense of rhythm is that it is a source of personal, private, divine inspiration. In every indigenous culture in the world, drums are used to connect the tribe and the individual to their definition of God. By playing repeated rhythms at a constant steady speed, the body goes into trance. Trance is a state in which we can talk to God.

Organized religion stresses the priorities of group participation for the sake of social and church agendas. The drum, as a divine tool, was taken out of the individual's hands, replaced with the middleman as interpreter of God's word. This change of religious imperatives placed the source of divine correspondence in an acceptable mode compatible with the evolving culture. The drum became unwelcome in complex cultures because of the private, personal connection that the player could achieve with God and the resultant lack of organized group participation. The irony is that drumming has always been a group effort in all indigenous cultures and a way for the group to establish a communication with their Divine cohorts.

A sense of rhythm is a sense of individual power if the rhythm is played properly at the right tempo or speed, with the right spaces between the notes, just the right way. The effect is like dialing a telephone number to the center of the universe. You are talking to God.

The sense of joy that comes from drumming is an overwhelming sensation because rhythm circumvents all the thinking, intellectual definitions of what is correct in life. The beat connects to the body. The brain is then infused with the momentum of life and is no longer held down by intellectual restraints. This event can be terrifying to experience if someone is afraid of losing control. It can also be very liberating.

The drum can be used in an infinite number of ways. It can be used to heal. The body responds to rhythm like a long-lost friend while the mind is soothed. The drum as an inspirational tool can be used in formal religious ritual whether it be Christian, Hindu, Shinto, Jewish, Muslim, Yoruban, or any other form of worship. And of course the drum can be used to invoke that most essential element of life, simple joy.

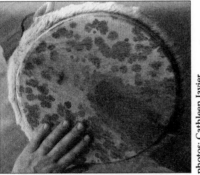

photos: Cathleen Javier

Hitting the drum in the center will produce a deep note. Higher-pitched tones result from striking the drum near the rim.

2

HOLES, DANCE, AND DREAMS

Any rhythm is made up of notes and non-notes. This is another paradox in drumming, much like life. The yin and yang of opposites is graphically portrayed in drumming as dance. There are notes and the spaces around the notes. The principles of the oriental martial art aikido are evident in the space, the "allowance" of rhythm to happen and change. The challenge to being a good drummer is to understand and respect the holes. The holes in a rhythm are opportunities for the body to respond. This becomes the dance. Drumming and dancing are partners, if the feel is there.

If one were to play all of the notes possible at any given moment, there would be no feel. It would be machine-like, with no sense of grace. There would also be a sense of chaos in the intensity. Here are the opposites of extreme order and its partner, chaos, waiting to happen just as soon as someone loses the beat in a drumming group where there is a strict

7

adherence to set patterns and approved parts. This can happen in authentic or traditional drumming. This kind of drum instruction is what most people think they have to learn before they become drummers. In reality you can learn all of the authentic rhythms and traditional rhythms only after you've learned how to feel rhythm in your heart and your body. Otherwise the sophisticated traditional rhythms will fall apart into chaos. In this different type of meditational, groove-oriented, conversational drumming there is enough space for the beautiful accidents of nature to happen. There is spontaneous appropriateness in whatever notes are played. It may not be authentic, but it feels good. There is also a sense of possible chaos in this type of drumming but at least we can deal with it in an ongoing and creative way without guilt. When certain notes are played and then certain holes or spaces allowed to appear, then you have a swinging, evocative, and danceable rhythm, and it doesn't matter whether it is authentic or not.

Meditative rhythms can be different from swinging dance rhythms, but they also have spaces which occur in certain parts of the pattern. The holes or spaces, not the notes, are the signals to the unconscious to let go, to trust the trance state and to journey. Putting the holes and the notes together in different ways around a basic pattern is what improvisation is about. Allowing the pattern to change yet stay connected to the original basic pattern is a progression from a naive state toward a wiser state of being. This is accomplished by following the rhythm instead of forcing the rhythm to obey your command. A pattern is not a static thing. Rhythm is alive, and it changes. Many times it changes unexpectedly, but the tempo and the downbeat must stay constant and steady. This constancy does not mean it is unchanging or boring. The constancy of feeling is a foundation on which we can build. The downbeat is the beginning note of a repeated pattern that everyone can agree on and use as an anchor to keep steady.

A computerized drum machine, on the other hand, does not change unless it is programmed to change. A human drummer responds to the moment, to the life that is coming through them and going on around them. Real drummers respond to life with subtle changes in the patterns. Even if the drummer abruptly stops, there is still rhythm. The momentum carries on through the silence and we can hear the rhythms that are always being played by the universe.

People are hungry today for the sound and feel of real drums in their lives. This is partly in response to the dominance of the electric drum machines in pop music for the last several decades. The human spirit has been inundated with an incessant facsimile of drumming that has not served the full purpose of drums in human culture. A very basic need has been forgotten. The actual experience of hand on skin and the vibrations from that encounter engender a healing state of being that is an ancient part of us.

When we experience this simple, basic hand-drumming process again, there is an inner voice that rejoices and says, "Finally! It's about time!" The healing of the spirit and the body can take place. In time.

Rhythm or "keeping time," as many musicians refer to playing in tempo, integrates the body with the mind in a nonintellectual way. The feel of the rhythm is physical and the mind then is not engaged directly. The use of a shaker or rattle in shamanic ceremonies entices the mind and diverts the intellect, while the deeper resonance of the drumhead occupies the

"How many drummers does it take to screw in a light bulb?"

"None. They got a machine that will do it."

—L.A. session musician's joke

body. The spine is encouraged to move, which we know now is very effective in the healing process.

Yoga and chiropractics encourage us to move. Certain kinds of chiropractic techniques, such as network chiropractics, actually allow the spine to undulate on its own, in waves. This can organically release trauma memory. The spine then readjusts itself in a fluidic way, much like yoga.

The bioelectrical life force, or Kundalini energy as it is referred to in Yoga, is generated at the base of the spine, in the lowest chakra, in the sacrum. Due to stress and the general trauma of life, this life energy sometimes does not take its intended trip up the spine to nourish and communicate messages to the brain. The creative force is then blocked from climbing up the spine. Yoga can release this energy flow. Chiropractics can also free up this flow inside the meningeal sheath by freeing up the locations of trauma memory. The locations of the life trauma memories are not only in the brain. They are also in the muscles where the trauma occurred and in other muscle groups that could or could not be obviously related.

The memories also reside in the meningeal sheath surrounding the spine. The meningeal sheath holds a saltwater solution that acts as a conducting medium for electrical information to pass up and down the spinal cord. Some modern chiropractic treatments have some success in clearing trauma memories located in the meningeal sheath. This envelope holding the saline solution connects to the sacrum at the base of the spine and then encloses the spine all the way up to the cranium where the same envelope encloses the brain. The saltwater carries electrical currents up and down the spine from the brain to the sacrum. The sacrum is a collection of small bones that ideally act as a pump. The cranium is also a collection of boney plates that ideally act as a pump of the meningeal fluid. Stress and trauma lock these natural pumps into calcified and rigid boney structures. The fluid does not flow readily. As a result, the electrical activity of the brain is not as acute—dim-witted, even.

The movement of the spine on its own accord frees up this rigidity so the flow of electrical activity to the brain is enhanced, even to the point of seeing God.

This is not to blaspheme. God is there, within us, and there are ways to get closer to that sensation, not only for the physical rush of feeling the life energy flow, but also for the innate wisdom that can flow into us while in that state of grace.

This wisdom is not intellectual. It comes from the body up to the brain. Not the other way around.

DANCE TO HEAL THE SPINE

"Let your backbone slip," is an old rock 'n roll lyric used to describe a state of freedom and joy. The lyric was possibly created by Big Joe Turner, the great blues shouter. He was a living legend who possibly even coined the term, "Rock 'n Roll." I was fortunate enough to record an album with him. I was called for the recording date in south-central Los Angeles in the mid-1970s. He settled his huge body down on a chair facing facing me, I sat at the drum set, and he gave me the tempo by tapping his cane on the floor.

"Here it is, Buddy." He struck the wooden floor with his cane until I picked up the beat. The rest of the band caught the groove and we cut the tune. Big Joe sat there with headphones on, his huge body sweating, working the beat with his improvised poetry. At the end, when we heard the playback, he looked at me and grinned.

"Buddy, you got that *beat* that the kids like to *dance* to!"

The rest of the band wasn't that interested in hearing the playback. We were getting a big $25 a track, so they were more intent on getting another tune in the can. I was soaking up what Joe was all about. The $25 bucks wasn't that important. To this day I still feel his presence in the drumming workshops when I talk and drum at the same time. I learned some of that ancient tradition of talking rhythm from him.

Big Joe was a walking, talking authority on the blues and also on this kind of healing energy. He was huge and getting old, but he could still be moved by the Spirit. References to "let your backbone slip" probably existed much earlier than Big Joe, because it is timely advice. Maybe there is an equivalent African phrase. Their drum patterns certainly encourage that movement. In the Deep South when I was a teenager I pondered the spiritual phenomenon in Black Southern Baptist churches where the devout were taken over by the Holy Spirit. There was usually a sudden jerking movement upward that whipped the person's spine like it was a wet noodle. Their head flew back and upward with the force of an electric jolt. These people weren't injured; they were being saved. Their spines were also being healed. This activity was brought on by the sermon, by the singing of the choir, and also by the banging of the tambourine. A good tambourine played by talented hands can engender a state of grace, just as a drum can. *The tambourine is a drum.* It was used by the women oracles at Delphi and by the shamans in the frozen tundra of Alaska and Siberia. It is the combination of a rhythmic hand on the skin head accompanied by the high-pitched jingling of small cymbals attached to the edges of the tambourine. This combination of lower drum sound and high frequency cymbals is for good reason cross-cultural. The human body responds to this combination in a trusting way.

Possibly we remember this combination from ancient times on a cellular level; an innate memory that dates back farther than history, back to the cave paintings or before. Maybe we feel a connection with the indigenous people surviving today who still use these tools. The sound of a drum head being struck and a cymbal clashed, or in pre-metallic times, to the sound of a shaker with shells were used to heal.

Ancient hunters were an essential part of the tribe or clan. When they came back from unsuccessful expeditions, gored and bruised, they sought shelter with their people and tried to

photo: Lynne Alexander

Workshop at *Seasons on Montana*, Cathy Javier's gift store in Santa Monica, California, and for many years the center for the author's drumming workshops.

let sleep heal them. While they slept, someone played the drum and shaker to scare away the bad memories, but also to bring the heart and body back into a peaceful balance. The soft tones of the drum, voice, and shaker seeping into the dreams of the hunters could have helped to heal them.

Drums and dreams are archetypal. The hunter and the hunted can combine in equilibrium and wholeness. The images painted on cave walls were an attempt to describe the spiritual comingling that the drum and the dream created.

This memory comes alive today in drumming groups and in individual rhythmic encounters. Memories of past lives involved with drums and rhythm are an area of rich imagery and imagination that can be accessed by a simple shaker and drum. There is no need for sophisticated playing to achieve this connection to our mystic mythic past. What is needed is a consistent beat that attunes the body and mind in a relaxed and safe manner. This act alone seems an heroic achievement in this modern age of speed, consumption, and competition.

3

LAYERS OF RHYTHM

The layering of rhythm is another workable analogy for living. We find ourselves trying to manage a number of different levels of activities at the same time. It doesn't have to be frustrating and stressful. Drummers do it all the time and it appears to be fun. At the foundation of life there is a simple large pulse. It can be called the "downbeat," for want of a better term. This large pulse is the origin of life. It is the impetus, the original intention for the groove of being.

The foundation rhythm is based on the downbeat of any pattern. It is the simplest form of that pattern, and the most important—the cornerstone to more complex rhythms. Drummers who play this basic rhythm are indispensible because all other variations are based on their downbeat. I encourage drummers to get comfortable with just working that big downbeat before they take off on trying to play the hot licks. This is also important for the drumming group. Without that solid downbeat, no one will have any fun because they won't be able to play together.

"Where's ONE?" some musicians may yell at the drummer because they cannot hear the downbeat. The "One" beat re-occurs every measure, such as "ONE, Two, Three, Four, ONE, Two, Three, Four, ONE, etc." repeated to the end of the song. Without knowing where "One" is, the lost player's improvisations sound wrong. They are without a tether to journey out-ward from in their improvisations. Normally hearing the down-beat enables them to return safe and sane to the basic original pattern at the end of their improvisations. Getting lost out there improvising with the Universe can be confusing and can create emotional turmoil if the creative pathfinder and the audience or dancers aren't brought back to earth in a coherent manner.

The rich diversity of life can be felt in the myriad rhythms laid over that basic downbeat. All musically orchestrated move-ment comes from the tacit agreement that all playing be based on the downbeat. Whatever type of player, no matter how good they think they are, must maintain their own inner sense of that downbeat—otherwise they cannot play with others. With-out that inner sense, they have yet to participate in the ensem-ble of life or in the joy of group improvisations of music and rhythm. Many intellectual players will lose their connection to the downbeat and rush off into more ephemeral, egotistical realms of improvisation, and then wonder why no one else is appreciating what a genius they think they are. They have lost the most essential connection to life; this umbilical connection to the beat and the group. The players who are locked into their own heads, no matter how technically proficient, will not get off because they are rushing and paying attention to only their own grand achievements. They're not feeling the groove that supports their own journeying. That groove comes from the group, as in the ensemble of life. Teamwork is essential.

Meanwhile, the player that stays oriented to that swing in the bottom end will always look good to the audience and to the other players and themselves, no matter how basically they play. They are acknowledging with every note that everyone else is also playing on the same groove.

The analogy of multiple layers of existence is demonstrated in the combinations of possible rhythms that work together. There is a simplistic assumption by some drummers that everyone must play exactly the same pattern to be correct. If this were the case, then drumming would be very boring. Rhythm is a living thing. It changes and grows under your hands as you play it. To try to control it, limiting its power, kills the energy that you are channeling. Balancing change with the need to maintain coherence is the challenge of drumming, as well as in living. The tapestry of multiple rhythms overlaying each other creates a dense orchestration of pulses. This is obvious in what early anthropologists called "primitive cultures" in Africa. The irony is that the scientists who were listening to these tribal rhythms assumed the rhythms were chaotic because they could not perceive the inspired organic fluidity of the multiple layers of orchestrated rhythms. Some of the Iba drum patterns of Africa are over twenty minutes long before they repeat. Without a willing ear, there is only a critic without appreciation. The challenge for our technological minds is to rediscover our own connection to rhythm. Without that connection, the mind is isolated in its own conceit. The mind is lost without the body that moves it and feeds it. The mind is not the domain of rhythm, yet it is very much influenced by rhythm and can be saved by it.

In our everyday lives the rhythms of our technological culture trick us into believing that each one of us must go faster, get there sooner, achieve more than the next person. This anxiety is unbiased. We are all affected by its mindless push that forces us into believing that there is no respite, no state of grace. The truth of our condition is something else entirely.

Group drumming brings total strangers into a harmony of participation, where they are smiling at each other for no other reason than they are having fun. The performance anxiety foisted upon us by the driving culture slips away and we perceive that grooves exist of and by themselves. They are not contingent on the stock market or who is in office. Grooves are eternal certainties that constantly fly in the face of current convention. To see someone get in touch with this is exhilarating for the teacher and the group. The person ceases to be concerned where they will be in the next hour. For that moment, they are playing the beat, paying attention to the next upcoming beat, not worried about making a mistake, laughing at their own abilities, and sharing in the cleansing rhythm that carries them outside of time and themselves. This is an active meditation with a biofeedback mechanism that tells you when you're doing it right. If the groove is there, if it swings, then you are in the correct meditative state.

Maybe one of the greatest paradoxes of drumming is what happens when we lose track of time. No matter how long you play, it becomes difficult, even impossible to determine exactly the length of time one has been drumming. This is an essential component of drumming as well as living. We lose ourselves in the moment, but more importantly, we lose our sense of the ticking clock. The appearance of sequential time disappears like the thin veil of illusion that it really is. By "keeping time," as the jazz players call it, we step outside of time.

This ability to eject our consciousness outside of linear time is one of the great values of drumming. It is a simple, cheap, and effective way to time travel. Its been done for centuries, right under the noses of technological societies, without their slightest understanding of the power that it generates. The assumption that "the primitives" drum and "lose their minds" is based upon the ignorance of being out of touch with rhythm. The shaman is literally carried away by the drumbeat, to journey into other realms. They go to the underworld and heal their patients, do battle with beings and forces that affect us here, and gain wisdom and knowledge of plants and animals that cannot be understood with words. This is all done with the help of the drum. There are more things in the Universe that cannot be talked about than there are words. Drumming is one way to articulate these things. By articulating them with rhythm, we know their names, and when we know their names, we have some power over them. Even better, we have some protection against their unspoken influence over our lives.

Ideally, drumming and rhythm can be perceived by the scientific community as a tool, but as we all know, "Teaching a pig to whistle is a waste of time, plus it infuriates the pig." I don't expect a breakthrough in the mainstream culture as yet.

ANXIETY AND THE BEAT

There are different sources of anxiety in drumming groups. One of the greatest sources of anxiety comes from a certain type of person that attends drumming groups and brings their performance anxiety with them. It can be women or men, but in this case there is a sad truth about the men. They have performance anxiety about everything—even having a good time. Some people realize that finding and *feeling* the groove is easy, but they have doubts about their own ability. Certain types of alpha men have the most difficult time finding the groove and locating the downbeat—let alone feeling anything. But they're sure they're very good at it, nonetheless. If they sense that they're not meshing with the group, they become embarrassed and hit harder and faster. They speed up the tempo, playing harder and faster, ignoring the downbeat, forgetting the constant pulse, intent on getting to the end, playing harder and faster—self-absorbed. Women have known this male malady for centuries. It is obvious in their lovemaking as well as in their headlong rush to cover the earth with concrete. When this problem is brought up in drumming groups, the women smile knowingly and the men grow red and get embarrassed—even angry.

A little boy tells his mom: "I wanna be a drummer when I grow up!"

His mother replies, "Honey, you can't do both!"

I was invited to a men's group in Atlanta, in a park at sunset. The ceremonial smudge stick was burned and the feather was used to purify all of them with the smoke. They forgot to "do me" and I asked for it so they apologized and smudged me too. They were very nice guys, intent on being as honest as was comfortable. They seemed to be professionals, all Anglo, and possessing some degree of higher education. Some were in their twenties, some were in their thirties and early forties—the Iron John generations.

I had done a drumming workshop the day before at a women's group north of Atlanta, in Roswell, Georgia. It was a mixed gender group and everyone seemed to stay with the beat and keep the tempo pretty steady, but this men's group in the park was different. After the men got smudged and formed into a circle on the ground, holding their drums and stones and other talismans, they shared their week with each other in a sort of light therapy. Finally the drumming was brought up.

They shared a group murmur, "Who's going to set the beat?" It was like I was the new gun in town. They knew I was fast, but they didn't know how fast. I was just curious how they did it so I didn't take control.

They asked me out of deference if I wanted to set the beat. I asked that they do what they had been doing and let me fit in. The fellow on the biggest djembe started a basic pattern and then the other men joined in. The tempo lasted for almost a minute before it began to speed up. Their expressions changed as they began their familiar acceleration process. Eventually, they broke a sweat and the drums were thundering across the park in a frantic roar that was speeding up and getting louder. They all began howling. Then they ended with a cacophonous anarchy of drum bashing. They chewed up my Egyptian doumbeks pretty good. Then they bonded and had a cigarette or whatever. One fellow wanted to buy the biggest djembe I could get. He didn't want a little sissy drum. I watched some African-American Atlanteans walking by at a respectable distance, squinting in our direction. They could have been thinking something like, "Oh no. The white guys are doing their drumming thing again."

But it doesn't matter what they thought. It was a good thing that we were drumming. Finding a groove is always a challenge, even for expert drummers, and there is no need to be embarrassed or angry at not being a certain kind of drummer. Everyone can find the steady rhythm in themselves. It's that steady pulse that we need, but are so fearful of. Sometimes it takes a while to find it.

The need for all of us to slow down, follow the beat, and ride the rhythm is important for our survival. The planet needs us to pay attention to the inner beat in ourselves. It is crying out for us to get with the beat and ride that flow. It is a way of reducing stress, of regaining wisdom and of sharing love.

When men or women get into a self-centered mode of thought, they rush the beat and fill up the spaces with neurotic noodling. The result is that no one else can play. There is no relaxed space between the big beats. The spaces are truly just as important as the notes—actually, the spaces are more important than the notes. When the holes are respected and left to live on their own, then rhythm becomes more than just notes, it becomes patterns. These patterns engender movement in the body of the listener and the player.

From a chiropractic point of view, this movement creates looseness in the spine, and this looseness releases trauma memory that is stored in the meningeal envelope surrounding the spine. The healing that occurs when the holes in the grooves are respected is a very important reason for everyone to listen, to not rush, not get anxious, and to let the rhythm carry the player.

Some people try to dominate the drum and the rhythm. Others tend to allow the rhythms into their beings—they meditate and take the inner journey with the drum. Some people play outward to the immediate world, to identify themselves with the thunderous sound, to work up a sweat, and to feel their bodies exerting power. Some people play to impress themselves, while underneath there is a fear. Maybe there was a time when the drums played in the night to scare away the beasts lurking just outside of the firelight.

Some people play the drum to invoke a state of grace in themselves—to invoke the creative energy of God or the Goddess in themselves, and to heal.

Some types of players tend to surrender to the groove quicker. This attitude of allowance rather than dominance lets the rhythm carry the players. Some people fear the groove, fighting against surrendering to the groove. For them, control seems to be an issue.

There are changes in a group of mixed gender. The flow finds an equilibrium that changes as the varying tempos invoke different dominant personalities. As a facilitator or drum coach, I feel that deciding where the groove goes gives everyone a sense of coherence. Warning against speeding up is somewhat like being a Kama Sutra teacher, keeping the groove in love and in life. And no one needs to dominate.

Of course all these things are generalities and quite laughable when taken on an individual basis. The point is that there are cultural influences on men and women that inhibit their ability to absorb the most healing aspects from rhythm. We all need all the help we can get.

In drumming, as in lovemaking, certain kinds of men get it wrong a lot of the time, from the women's point of view. Not speeding up is one of the biggest challenges for men. They're much more focused on learning the pattern, getting the hand technique correct, focusing on playing the right sequence of notes on the correct hand. Women generally get into the groove and stay there. Some women have these "male" problems too, primarily because they're caught up in the same illusion of the technological culture that they have to be the best at something, that they have to exhibit some ability, in order to prove themselves. They have this anxiety based on childhood trauma or family expectations, or cultural brainwashing. Whatever the reason, the challenge now is to feel the wisdom that comes up in our selves when we combine our energies and stay on the groove. I hear amazing rhythms come up through people who have never been trained, but are allowing themselves to play from this physically creative and intuitive place. It is as if there are generations of drummers wanting to play through these willing novices, if they'll keep their intellect out of the way and just play. Channeling Gene Krupa is not really out of the question.

Generations of drummers have come and gone who still play rhythms. If one is so inclined, these energies can be invoked. There are Gods who are drummers. The Santeria religion is a mix of African Yoruba, slavery, and Spanish Catholicism. The deities (Orisha) are invoked with the drums. Mention *I Love Lucy* and the song "Babalu" comes to mind. This is actually an invocation to the Santeria Orisha, and it was sung live to millions of Americans. This blessing was bestowed on us by the great drummer and band leader, Desi Arnaz, and we didn't even know it.

A SENSE OF HUMOR HELPS

Gene Krupa was a great big-band drummer. This is a story about his ongoing feud with his greatest competitor, Buddy Rich.

When Gene Krupa Died

When the great big-band drummer Gene Krupa died and went to Heaven, he was greeted at the Pearly Gates by St. Peter. St. Peter was effusive. "Wow! Gene Krupa! We're really glad to have you here in Heaven!" St. Peter was graciously generous. "Your drums are set up over on Cloud Nine. Your white, pearl-finish Slingerlands with the twenty-six-inch bass drum. Just make yourself at home, Mr. Krupa. Anything you need, just let me know."

Krupa was flattered, but he hesitated, "Before I come in, Pete, there's one question. Is Buddy Rich up here?"

St. Peter was shocked. "Of course not, Gene."

"Good. We don't get along too well." Gene said, and came on into heaven.

So Gene Krupa went over and sat down behind his white pearl Slingerland drumset and started to loosen up his wrists. Suddenly he heard all these Buddy Rich drum licks thundering from behind a big white cloud. He became very upset and called to St. Peter. "Hey Pete! I thought you said Buddy Rich wasn't up here!"

St. Peter assured him quickly, "That's not Buddy Rich, Gene. That's God. Sometimes he pretends he's Buddy Rich."

This story is not intended to impugn anyone or anything, including God or Buddy Rich. The point is that drumming is fun and a powerful medium of inspiration. Even the Gods are drummers.

Fifteen-year-old Buddy met Big Band leader and drummer Gene Krupa in 1964.

A True Story about Buddy Rich

When Buddy Rich went in for a brain tumor operation, the anesthesiologist asked him, "Mr. Rich, is there anything you're allergic to?"

He grinned that huge white set of choppers at her, "Only country and western music."

This is not a put-down of country and western music. I love to play country and I love to play western. It is all great music and it all has the truth in it. The feels or grooves are universal. The body and mind, moving to rhythm, can dance and heal, even in cowboy boots.

Wawe Aba. The Wawe seed of the hardwood tree is used for carving drums.

4

BASH AND HOWL

The reasons for drumming are as numerous as there are drummers. Everyone approaches rhythm from their own individual point of view and experience. Every person has their own unique sense of rhythm and they express it in their own distinct style. What is truly miraculous is that everyone can play rhythm together. All rhythmic patterns have some commonality that crosses all kinds of boundaries. Music is the universal language, and rhythm is the spoken word of that language.

"What good is the answer to the Universe if you can't dance to it?" is a rhythm and blues Zen Koan. It might have been used by George Clinton of Parliament Funkadelic, among others. There is wisdom in the rhythmic feel that goes beyond words.

There seem to be cultural and gender rhythms, although there are no restrictions based on those categories. The only restrictions seem to be in the minds of the beholders. In some men's drumming groups there is a tendency to drum for different reasons than women's drumming groups. In my experience, some men drum for outward reasons: distraction, to make noise, to scare away the beasts in the night, to communicate to other tribes, to get off, to break a sweat and feel the physical rush of playing hard, to impress women or other men.

Some women's groups tend to play drums for more internal reasons: to get in touch with their inner sense of creativity, to find peace, to heal, to feel joy, to gain confidence, or lose their sense of self and merge with a greater consciousness.

Of course all these different reasons can be gender reversed based on the individual. There are no rules to finding and playing the grooves.

One phenomenon I've already mentioned, found primarily in men's groups, is that they tend to start drumming at a slow tempo, then play louder and faster until they are at the top of their physical endurance and speed. Then they howl and cheer and bond in whatever way men like to bond. I call this the "Bash and Howl" school of drumming. This is great fun. It also seems to be a very male thing to do; get the pattern started, then speed up until they get off, then go outside and have a cigarette.

My first drum teacher was a woman, Eileen Trafford, in Elkhart, Indiana. I was eight years old. She taught me among other things, the importance of constancy. She had me sight read difficult percussion music, and play to a metronome. This prepared me for a career as a percussionist in orchestras, drum and bugle corps, jazz, rock 'n roll, rhythm and blues, and session recording. The common factor in all music is the constancy of tempo and the attention to the downbeat. For people not exposed to that type of discipline, keeping a steady beat is not perceived as of primary importance. I have come to realize over the years that when tempo is steady, a commonality of consciousness appears in the dancers, the listeners, and the players that is much greater than the sum of the individual parts. This is a key element in mystical drumming among indigenous cultures around the world. In Native American drumming ceremonies, the speed of the pulse is critical to the intended effect. The same is true in Bali, Indonesia, India, and in any culture that uses rhythmic drumming for ceremony, meditation, ritual, and magic.

Drumming is an active meditation that can free us from the normal pressures of living too. The brain is occupied in unusual ways as a part of this meditation. Our attention is split up in order to deal with the various drumming tasks that are assigned to different parts of the body. The brain is not really the controlling entity. The body as a whole seems to be in control. It is a holographic approach to task management.

When I play in a group, I tap a tambourine with my foot on the downbeat to hold everyone together. I'm also hitting the drum, listening to the group, using a shaker with one hand, as well as talking too much. My attention moves around quickly to monitor all of these events, but it does not stay very long at any one location. If I did, the process would stop.

Most people may believe that their attention span is a one-dimensional skill capable of concentrating on only a single thing at a time, to the exclusion of all other things. In drumming we see quite graphically that attention can be broken up and assigned to different hands and legs at the same time, in a multilevel process. This is a working model of micromanagement, if you want to see it in those terms.

While playing a drum during a seminar or workshop, I am usually talking to the other drummers, tapping my foot on a tambourine, while both of my hands are performing unique syncopated rhythms. I am also explaining the phenomenon of drumming in a lucid nonrhythmic style. People sometimes are amazed at all of this simultaneous activity. For me it is a state of grace. It is like I am playing with the Gods, or John Coltrane. I feel as if every part of me is being used. It is a fantastic workout. I always feel better after a drumming group session, no matter what the other players do, because I am lost in this multiple method of meditation.

Sometimes I am amazed too, but at that moment when I am impressed with my own achievements, the process stops. I become fixated and I lose the beat because my attention stops moving. I get stuck on myself. In reality "I" am not creating this flow of musical rhythm and lucid discourse. The "I" is merely trying to stay out of the way. That's why the greatest of players, like John Coltrane, always insist that they are just letting the creativity flow through them; that they are the humble vessels of this inspiration. I truly enjoy this feeling of being occupied to the fullest of my abilities. The secret of all this multiple tasking is that I don't panic and focus on one thing. I keep moving my attention to different spots of activity just long enough to check it, then I move on to the next station; my right hand, my left hand, my right foot, my left foot, my mouth, and then my ears, to see if what I'm doing and saying makes sense on an intellectual and aesthetic level. In drumming schools this process is called "independence," being able to do different things with both hands and both feet all at the same time. It's quite fun, and it can also be a transcendant process.

The underlying reason that we are able to do this juggling of tasks is that we do not fixate on any one event or process. This is based on a concept that is quite cosmic; that nothing

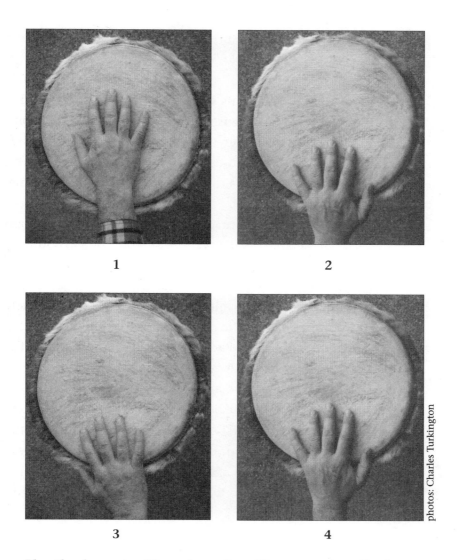

1

2

3

4

photos: Charles Turkington

Play the drum steadily and evenly, with an accent on the down-beat "1" in the middle of the drumhead, with no hesitation before repeating the phrase. Alternating hands is important in waking up your sleeping hand.

is more important than anything else. There is no evaluating going on. No judging. No inner critic getting in the way. We just exist to be playing all these things at the same time. We become all the beats. This same mental and physical process is applicable in life. A sense of panic is usually what stops us from doing the intuitively correct thing during a split second decision. Getting fixated on our own achievements inhibits the flow that would take us on to the next meaningful achievement.

What this does to the brain is most interesting. First, it gives us a new model for task management in our lives. It shows us a way to juggle different assignments in our lives without feeling overwhelmed. The brain is quite capable of handling many different functions at the same time. The trick is to not pay too close attention to any of them. That does not mean that we are unconscious of errors. Rather, it means that we don't get caught up with being self-conscious about errors. The biggest pitfall for drummers who are getting pretty good is that they impress themselves with a beat, and actually say to themselves, "Wow! That's really great!" And then they lose it. This self-consciousness slows down, or even stops, the creative process. It demonstrates how slow and cumbersome the brain is when compared to what the body can do when it is not impaired by its own self-consciousness and ego. So when the drumming gets hot and heavy, and licks are being traded back and forth as fast as lightning bolts, don't listen to yourself. Listen to everything. And especially don't be impressed by what you or anyone else is doing or trying to do. That will slow you down and hinder the group from feeling that all-important down-beat and staying on a steady, constant rhythm.

5

THE GODS LIKE TO DANCE

Rhythm frees the listener and the player from the usual linear way of perceiving reality. By keeping time, the drummer is freed from time. This is another great paradox of drumming.

After playing a drum pattern for awhile, it is hard to tell just how long it has been going on. The perception of time is changed; it is distorted and stretched. The player gets outside the "if-then" mode of thinking about life: "If I do this, then this will happen." In rhythm, things happen, but not necessarily in a linear sequence. Ideas in rhythmic improvisation can come up, then disappear, then come up later in a different way that takes the player on a new path of investigation. By riding the beat, the player is taken away, yet arrives back where they began—hopefully richer with a new experience.

This ability to step outside of day-to-day events is one of drumming's most seductive and liberating characteristics. The drummer realizes that the world is not dictated by the clock. It is not controlled by the people who want everyone to get in line. The world is actually an ephemeral place that changes appearances with the slightest breeze of rhythmic variation.

When the beat is going, it is the most powerful thing at that moment. An undefinable, magical environment is created by the tone of the drum. I see this happen every time we have a drumming workshop at our store on Montana Avenue in Santa Monica, California. The evening strollers are usually intent on window shopping, or showing off their babies or their new wardrobe. In general it is a conservative street, but when the passersby come within hearing of our drumming group they stop outside and listen for a moment, then a small grin will appear on their otherwise stoic faces and then a bit of movement is discernible somewhere in their bodies. They actually break down and smile before moving on down the street. Just a moment earlier they would not have thought it possible or even desirable to exhibit such an obvious reaction. This mystical effect carries out to the edges of the sound space made by the drumming. When people come into contact with that space of tonal rhythm, they are subject to its mysterious and healing effects. Within this special space there can be profound healing and joy.

This quality may be one reason why Africans who were enslaved could survive such harsh treatment. The rhythms they brought with them gave them sustenance, strength, and patience in their suffering. We are still enslaved, but a portion of our soul can be set free. This is not in a metaphorical way, but in a very real way. The perceptions of the player as well as the listener are freed of physical restraints while a sense of power is generated in the heart and soul.

When I help people start to play, I try to make the point that these rhythms come from cultures that were considered unimportant, even inferior, by our dominant society. Now that we, the members of this dominant culture, desire to learn these rhythms there is also a need for an atonement for what has happened to the cultures where these rhythms originated. It is all well and good that we want to play these rhythms, but we must understand the suffering that has happened and is still happening to these indigenous cultures. These rhythms come from the earth and the people, from their food and work, as well as their religion. Some of those cultures are being wiped out as you are reading these words. The temptation to take these rhythms and use their power without also respecting the people is a great tendency in our technological culture. We take and use without thinking of where the item originated. This kind of thievery can backfire, especially with sacred items. I have heard stories of bad luck visiting those who want to hold on to these objects of power, mistakenly thinking that they are impervious to the mystical effects of the artifact, or the attendant Karma. Rhythms are also artifacts that have power. They require humbleness and respect for them to work their good medicine. They can free us and show us a larger perspective of our world.

If you're not smiling, you're not doing it right.

Today we live as slaves to our technological environment. We are harangued into believing that consumerism is the only way to survive, that we must submit our souls and bodies to a form of corporate slavery. This illusion can be broken by playing a drum. Even more amazing is that drumming in a corporate environment creates a sense of teamwork that is far more effective than most company seminars.

We drum and become connected to a larger sense of well-being in the Universe where healing, light, and energy come into our bodies from the source of life, not the source of oppression and death. This may sound awfully anarchistic, but we let ourselves succumb to the illusion that life is bleak and joyless; that work and bill-paying is our only reality. There is another reality within reach where we could be dancing. That reality can be made real in a moment's notice just by playing a drum, by feeling the beat and dancing. All indigenous cultures have known this. As a technological culture we must relearn it in order to save our souls and keep the world from graying out.

The fear of the oppressor is that this sense of freedom will break the illusion of control over us. We must heal the oppressor, which is ourselves. We drive ourselves to death. It may be in a nice shiny new car but the destination is still the same. The alternative is to feel a sense of connectedness to the rhythms of nature that give us joy and healing power. That healing power is contagious. We can heal others as well as ourselves just by feeling the connection to our rhythmic selves.

We all have a sense of rhythm; it is just covered over by the culture, by childhood trauma, by fear of being the fool, by fear of the unknown, but our innate sense of rhythm is still there. The unknown aspects of what rhythm can do is a very mysterious realm of discovery for the drummer. This can also be a most rewarding state of mind.

One of my older students, a grandmother, thanked me for "making the rest of her life worth living" because she had started from scratch and became a "Fearless Improvisor" on her drum. She sat in her apartment, alone, and was excited by what she was doing. Her drum carried her away. She also organized a group of grandmothers who all play together.

We have not only a responsibility to ourselves to play and feel rhythm, but also a responsibility to the world and the Universe. By freeing ourselves through rhythm, we become a member of a greater whole—a whole that has been there all the time. Rhythm is life itself. By playing we connect to what is important.

The Universe is waiting for us to play. It needs us to play because the Gods like to dance. As individuals and in groups we articulate the beat that is life, awakening the life force in all things. A sense of rhythm is a sense of life and rejuvenation that is essential to a well-balanced, integrated, successful partnership with life. And it's fun too. If you're not smiling, you're not doing it right.

Community: We don't fight over the same food when we have the same stomach.

(Adinkra proverb)

photo: Cathleen Javier

Seasons, "The Most Unusual Gift Store," 1021-A Montana Avenue, Santa Monica, CA 90403. Drumming workshops Tuesday and Friday nights, 7:30 'til 9:00 P.M. Everyone is invited!

6

THE BIG BEAT

People coming to the drum with a technologically oriented mind assume rhythm is a black and white set of values; that playing on the beat is all that's correct. Our inner critic is very comfortable with looking at the world in this simple way.

In actuality, on the beat is not such an exact place to play. Some people who are intently watching the beat actually hit the beat too soon or too late. They probably anxiously over-anticipate many other things in their lives too. This style of drumming comes across as an impending sense of doom, as if the rhythm will fall apart if the drummers fail in their attempts to nail the downbeat correctly. They fear that their wrong notes will throw everyone else off and break the rhythm. This fear injects a sense of anxiety into the drumming group, often resulting in a forced and labored drumming experience for everyone in the group, but especially for the person who is unaware that they are the cause of the problem. They are so worried about staying on the beat that they throw the rest of the group into a struggle for rhythmic balance and fluidity. This is offset by the person who just plays, who does not impart anxiety, but just continues to support the group's groove by not worrying.

"Don't panic when you lose the beat," is good advice for most drummers. Here's a big secret about great drummers; even the best drummers get lost. The difference between the experienced drummers and the novice is that there is no self-recrimination in the seasoned drummer. There may be just a microsecond of a pause for the seasoned drummer to locate the downbeat again, then they are back on the road, playing away without stopping and saying, "Wait! I made a mistake!" It is not an important issue. It is a transitory event of no consequence. There are no mistakes in this kind of drumming; it might even be an interesting variation. You just need to let your body do what it knows how to do, without the inner critic trying to stay in control. The important thing is to keep the beat going. This can be a good habit to acquire in life too: to keep moving when we have to and not stop the band when life throws an unexpected curve at us.

There is an interesting effect when a drumming group gets into the uncomfortable situation I've just described. When things sound the worst—the musicians are not in sync at all, and they're just continuing to play, hoping that it will get better—something happens. The beat falls apart, and then it comes back together again—like a resurrection. Everyone begins to focus on what is happening in the group instead of their own playing. When the feel becomes coherent again, everyone notices it and they all usually break into smiles. There is a new feeling of relaxed energy pulling everyone along, taking them to a higher level. So the mistakes were actually necessary for everyone to get over their fear of making a mistake! The reestablished feeling shows us that there can be hope for whatever is next, just when things sound the worst. All that is needed is to be easier on ourselves when we crash and burn, trying a rhythm that isn't quite appropriate or when there is a psychological barrier that someone must overcome. Getting back on the beat is akin to getting back in the saddle after being thrown from a horse, but with drumming it happens much quicker and it doesn't hurt. Just get back on the beat and keep riding. No blame, no shame.

"Getting lost" is an abstract concept. There is a forest of different variations of any rhythm. A drummer who is improvising chooses a variation at any given point, not just from an intellectual memory bank of playable "licks," but also from an intuitive source that doesn't reside in the brain. There are different kinds of improvising. One style takes into consideration what the basic pattern feels like so that the improvised notes fit into the basic pattern. Another type of improvising is where the soloist uses a learned "lick" and plays it whenever he or she gets the courage up to cut loose. This second type of soloing is not conducive to maintaining the groove. It usually feels like someone is phoning in their part from some other city. It's not a part of the group feel. The type of improvising where there is a conversation-like give and take between the various players is an exciting method of soloing. It's the style I have come to believe a lot of people are looking for in a drumming group experience.

This conversation with drums starts tentatively, then grows to a quick back and forth exchange between the players, each adding comments on their own but always staying in touch with the original basic feel. In the Gospel churches this "Call and Response," where the preacher calls out and the members of the congregation respond with encouragement, is a magical process that brings everyone closer together and to a higher sense of communion with the Divine. The same effect happens in the drumming groups, but it takes a willingness to throw it down without fear and to encourage others to do the same, all the while keeping the beat going.

There is a physical memory of rhythm in the hands and arms, the hips, the back, the feet, the shoulders, the buttocks. That is what we strive to connect to as drummers. When we lose the beat, it is usually because the brain has taken over again and our attention wanders from our bodies.

Sometimes, a drummer can lose the basic pattern because they're doing a variation that is so far away from the original pattern that they have to stop for a microsecond and reestablish the beat in their own heads. That is when the group is important for the soloist. The hardest job in the group is to play the simplest part because that is the one beat that is most needed. Being consistent and repetitive on a drum is not to everyone's liking.

Some people have an underlying anxiety about the mundane that forces them to play more notes, to rush the beat for fear of getting bored. They lack the ability to stay focused. Psychologists may label it "attention deficit disorder" (ADD) or some other diagnosis. Drumming groups can help this type of habitual mental straying because drumming is an active meditation. It is a perfect biofeedback machine. We know when we are on the beat, and we know when we have strayed, because the feel is not there. Getting back to the beat shows our wandering attention a way to reconnect to the ongoing event. We acquire a method to pay attention to our attention. The meditation grows out of the joy with every beat that we play; we pay attention to what we are playing on every beat because it is exciting, not because we *must*, which is the way many meditative disciplines are taught.

This mindset can be likened to a yuppie virus. The person becomes so intent on owning a new thing, they concentrate so deeply on it, that they lose their sense of self. It is a way to avoid the sense of self and the work that may need to be done there. Then they are distracted by something else when the charge of newness wears off. Drumming is a method of finding your self. For someone to think that they'll get it if they force it to their will, or if they play more notes than someone else, or get to the end before everyone else, having played more notes than anyone else, is missing the point. It can't be possessed or thrown away.

The drumming process can be a vehicle for enlightenment. This kind of enlightenment is nonverbal, so any of the intellectual functions will be frustrated in trying to define it, but it speaks in a wisdom that your soul and body understand.

Playing on the beat is not the law, though. In playing directly on the beat a very focused, attention-oriented feel is created. This is used in orchestral music and military marching bands or flamenco dancing where precise organization is important.

Playing behind the beat creates a different effect. This style of playing is more relaxed, very fluid and forgiving. This style can be found in the best of Rhythm and Blues, Rock 'n Roll, Folk, Caribbean, Reggae, New Orleans "Second Line," Delta Blues, Country Blues, and many other personal styles of music.

I was classically trained from the age of eight and it took me many years to unlearn the intellectual, elitist assumptions

"Mindful mindlessness." For drummers, it is a familiar state of being.

about playing in tempo. When I met great musicians who could play without a sheet of manuscript paper in front of them, I realized that there was another source of inspiration separate from and much deeper than the classical training that I had received. I thank my teachers for giving me an open mind toward the inspired playing sometimes called "Ignorant Genius." It is really playing from the heart—the kind of music that inspires and moves the listener. Correctness is not an issue with this kind of music. Tempo will vary, a twelve-bar blues tune will become a fourteen-bar blues pattern, then change again to something else. The mystery of the feel is what compels us to pay attention to the soul of the music and forget about what is correct.

"Feel" is an elusive, yet magical, ingredient that has many spiritual and psychological requirements that cannot be learned by the mind of the player. This talent is assimilated by our bodies and our hearts.

WHERE'S THE BEAT?

"Laid back" is a term used to describe playing behind the beat, or "back in the pocket" as some Southern players refer to it. That's where the fun is. Intellectual players seem to fear playing just slightly behind the beat because they need to feel that they are in control, and they hate the concept of being late. Once this anxiety is noticed and compensated for, the intellectual player can finally relax and find the groove, but it will be an intellectual exercise until they can really understand this lateness as the truly right way to play.

In a sense, our modern cultures have been playing right on the beat and even in front of the beat for centuries—pushing us faster. This underscores our sense of mission and accomplishment as a culture, but it also creates a driven, neurotic, mindless, bodiless momentum, as in the difference between aerobics and actual dancing. Leave it to the modern mind to take the fun out of dancing and turn it into work. When the beat is relaxed, the body has a chance to move in a more natural manner. This subtle change creates a deeply healing and safe environment for our hearts and minds.

Playing behind the beat is a great art form in itself among great musicians. Only the players with maturity and understanding can work in this realm. The players who don't relax are just that, they are only players. They aren't the real thing, no matter how many notes they can play.

This psychology of back in the pocket is definitely inherent in the blues. This style of working the beat comes from Africa, with a side trip through the Southern part of the United States. This is part of what makes the music of this country so wonderfully universal.

One of the original purposes of writing music down in an accepted manuscript form was a need for commonality. A composer in Vienna could be assured that his music would be performed correctly in the courts of France or England or some other distant venue. The musicians who could read the manuscript form of music were the ones who worked. They became professional musicians. This intellectual approach to performance created a schism in the world of music between the ones who could read versus the ones who could not read but yet could play. The amazing thing about rhythm and music is that it is not necessary to be trained to play. You only need the desire and the ability to listen and to learn. And hopefully, the humility to be taught.

The ironic thing about popular music is that the manuscript sheet music of something like Little Richard's "Tutti Frutti," the great rock 'n roll song, can only tell us the notes played. The written music cannot tell us what the feel is like. It cannot tell us the most important ingredient of the composition. It can only state something like, "Con Brio,"or "to be played at a brisk tempo." Little Richard probably would never use that description. "Just rip it up" might be more likely.

In the case of this song, "Tutti Frutti," the tempo is very fast—frantic even. Yet the feel is not rushed. It is in the pocket. The best players have the ability to play fast, yet still play behind the beat, so here is another paradox. Playing fast, yet behind the beat, is a form of rhythm that cannot be totally explained, but it can be felt. Fast and relaxed. In martial arts this is also a desired state of performance. As Muhammed Ali said, "Float like a butterfly, sting like a bee."

So the beat is not a digitally correct location in musical cosmology. The beat is not really on or off. The beat becomes a fat, living entity that responds more like a round waterbed being kicked down a country road, rather than a Lambourgini that is humming along perfectly on the infomercial highway. There is a sense of loose fun. This is a great secret that exists beyond the world of trained music. It is the genius of great performers who have the authority to play around the beat and do not always need to read the notes they are so magically creating.

Currently attending the workshops is a woman who is blind. She has fallen in love with playing the drums, and her joy is evident to everyone else. Her seeing-eye dog lies patiently next to her while she taps on a djembe and grins. She is also a classically trained vocalist and pianist, but the drum gives her something that she has been hungry for outside of the classical realm. She doesn't have to "think" to play it, although old habits are hard to break. She wanted to "learn" all of the authentic rhythms so that she could play with her friends who are trained musicians. I encouraged her to find the rhythms that could work with a variety of styles of music. Authentic African rhythms wouldn't necessarily work behind pop tunes, although there might be a hint of that original pattern in the ditty on the radio that you tap your finger to. It has been changed, however, by the mingling of cultures here in the United States This woman could naturally play along with just about any kind of music, but her mindset insisted that she be properly trained. This actually prevented her from playing. Her natural ability was overwhelmed by her need to feel correct. This is a common state for most of us. When she just played and listened to the rhythm, she learned what she wasn't expecting to learn—which was more about what her ears were tuning out than anything else. She found the syncopated beats that weren't normally part of her musical training. These are the beats that are hitting on odd places, on the upbeats.

The upbeats aren't something we're familiar with. They may hit in odd spots, but we can still feel them. They feel good. Its just that we can't always hit them correctly because we've been overtrained in stricter rhythmic patterns that don't use upbeats. The syncopated upbeats are what gives any rhythmic pattern its individuality. It is the nuance of rhythm, its the spice in the gumbo of American music. If we approach playing these unusual upbeats as part of a learned rhythm, we often don't feel that rhythmic pattern. We only parrot what's been fed to us. That is a passive, brain-intensive kind of learning. The other kind of learning trains the attention of the learner on how that particular syncopation hits in context to the downbeat and the overall pattern. Then the player gets a feel of how their own notes fit into the groove. This is more interactive than learning a pattern note-perfect, and then just repeating it until you think you've had enough. The meditation comes with the attention to every note and how it falls in relation to the overall pattern and feel. This form of meditation is nonintellectual.

Many disciplines of meditation strive for this state of mindful mindlessness. For drummers, it is a familiar state of being.

photos: Charles Turkington

Djembe (left), and Ashiko (right) drums with goatskin heads, handcarved in Ghana.

7

THE HEALING

When our bodies feel the tones of a hand drum being played, a deep memory begins to emerge. The body recognizes the familiar vibrations, welcoming those sounds and feelings as a long-lost friend. Since ancient times, in many cultures, drums have been played for healing. Why this simple tool is used with such subtle results is a great question that has been studied in many indigenous cultures, but is just being discovered in our society. There are many different rhythms for evoking trance states.

The human abdominal cavity responds to drumhead vibrations as if it were receiving an internal massage, although the effect could be more abusive depending on the speed, volume, and intensity. Our craniums respond in the same manner.

Drumming has been equated with violence, but in reality what is needed is a judicious amount of force to create a good tone. Much like aikido, again, too much force will defeat you.

The hand hits too heavy, which muffles the drumhead, making the tone less distinct so the novice hits it harder, making even less sound. A lighter touch brings the sound up and out of the head, making it easier to play more subtle rhythms. This quality of rhythmic tone creates a healing environment for the body and the mind. We feel safe in this tonal and rhythmic environment.

The body seems to remember and respond to the tones of the healing drum with a sense of relief. Maybe the genetic memory connects to ancient prehistory activities in a clan or tribe where a woman beat a drum for the returning hunters, so they could lie down and heal their wounds after failing to kill food. Maybe the woman was a seer in a cave while the others slept, ate, had sex, or painted pictures on the cave walls. The sleeping hunters—hungry and delirious from lack of food, sore, cut, and bruised from trying to hunt, getting attacked, even gored—dreamed of the animals. Their ears and bodies absorb the safety of the cave, the warmth of the fire, and the heartbeat of a drum, softly accompanied by a chant for good luck, a message to the spirits of the trees, the forest animals, the sky, the moon.

Their dreams blend animal with human. They are connected as we could never understand, a communal consciousness owning members of humans, animals, plants, and elemental forces. There is a belongingness where requests for understanding are answered in symbols. The dream animals are painted on the cave walls, studied, and talked to. Scared and hungry, early humans needed the drum to keep away the night and to feel included in the mystery of life.

Healing also comes from other aspects of the drum. As a power tool, the mere action of hitting a drum and getting a good tone out of it is a massive achievement for some people who have been traumatized. A somber young couple in their twenties came into our shop, passing time while they were waiting for their table at a restaurant across the street. The young man saw the standing drum and wanted to hit it. His hand hovered over the head, full of ambivalence. Should he?

"Go ahead and hit the drum." I said. "That's what it's for."

He gave it a tentative pat. Inconclusive.

"Hit it harder. You won't break it." I coaxed.

He gave it a whack and the deep tone filled up the small shop. He immediately grinned, as did his date. He reacted with such enthusiasm after just one stroke that I wanted to see him play some more, but the couple shared that one drum note as if it were their first drink of water on the desert after a long trek. They crossed back to their waiting table, both much happier than when they had come into the shop.

In a sense, our culture has been starving us of the refreshment of rhythm. We have been fed a strict diet, devoid of natural rhythmic supplements. Pop music has been using electronic drums for so long we have lost the memory of what real drums feel like. Even on recorded music, there is a difference between electronic drum machines and the real drummer. The effect of the real drums can still be felt, even on a record or CD. That's why a lot of people who are non-drummers are starting to hit a drum themselves. If that's the only way to get the effect, then do it yourself.

The makers of drum machines have attempted to program into the circuits the ability to vary in degrees the speed of the different notes. They have a button called "Quantize." A songwriter using a drum machine can compute out a simple drum part for a song, but it doesn't feel like the real thing! The melody may be mellifluous, the chords may be killers, even the bass part may be a groovy thing, but damn! That drum part sounds like a typewriter. Too incessant, irritating. So, by pressing this little button that the designers in their white lab coats have put on there, the erstwhile composer jiggles up the electronic signals just a little bit and the drum part almost sounds natural. It has inserted random microsecond variations between the notes, so the drum part is no longer correct, but it sounds more natural. The other things missing from this artificial drum part are the emotional and physiological effects that real drums have on the mind and body of the listener. Also missing is the attitude of a real drummer, the reason most composers today use the drum machine. Real drummers aren't always cooperative or available to play the same thing over and over for hours on end, unless they get paid.

Rhythm, in its natural state, changes all the time.

The main reason drum machines were invented was time. Time is money when you're in the recording studio. It takes the engineer more time to mic the drums properly than any other instrument—at least an hour. Every drum on a drumset has its own tonal frequency, the microphones need to be positioned properly to get the right overtones. If the drummer hits too hard, the tone changes and the mics can't handle the sound, so another take is needed. The drums have to be isolated in a booth so that they don't bleed onto the other tracks of instruments. That's expensive when the rates are sometimes into the hundreds of dollars per hour. The main studios always allow a setup time for the drummer too, which affects the money flow for the studio somewhat. All in all, it is a real pain to capture the true sound of drums, especially when it gets delegated to the back of the mix of a song, where it is not really featured, just felt.

I was recording some sessions in the early seventies, before drum machines were invented. A metronome was the only time-keeping mechanism at that time, and there was really no way to use it effectively in the studio. The drummer who could keep a steady tempo worked more than the flashy guys. If other players had to overdub to a basic drum track that speeded up or slowed down, then they had problems fitting in their own little bits of genius. The steady pulse was essential for guitar players, horn players, keyboard players, and singers, to pace their own performance in the overdubbing. The irony of it is that while playing live, simultaneously, all these different players did not mind that the tempo speeded up or slowed down slightly. It added to the emotional effect of the tune. They all did it together so it felt comfortable—unless one individual wasn't paying attention. That of course led to arguments during the breaks.

"Hey, stupid! You're rushing the beat!" or, "Pick up the beat! We're dying up here!" may be yelled by a paranoid singer who thinks that a faster tempo will make him sound better. Usually just the opposite is true. Slow down the groove, relax, have fun. Don't let them see you scared. Don't panic. Drummers often become the transactional analyst for the band—but in the studio, the machines took over. They ruled.

The recording equipment was very expensive, so producers and players reluctantly had to surrender the feel to the limitations of the technology. A drummer or percussionist who speeded up or slowed down was not technologically dependable.

The drum machine was developed by people who made computers. An internal clock decided the tempo or speed of the drum pattern. Fancy knobs and buttons dazzled the simple-minded technicians who spent great amounts of time programming in drum parts that sounded artificial and sterile, but were dependable. Plus the machine did not have an attitude like a real drummer.

"If you don't like the way I play, then play it yourself!"

I grew up playing to a metronome; sight reading very difficult drum music while obeying a metronome. Eileen Trafford, my first drum teacher, was a wonderful teacher but a stern taskmaster. She trained me for six years in orchestral percussion, rudimental drumming, jazz, and theory. As a result, I acquired rock-solid meter. Meter is the speed at which the music is being performed. I had played for so many years to a metronome it was like I had one imbedded in my head. I did one session at Capitol Records for a friend of mine, the old folk artist, Vince Martin, from Coconut Grove, Florida. It was unusual in that he sang his song and added a number of verses that he didn't want in the final album version. He was improvising on the spot. The muse was with him, so he let the flow carry him; in the old tradition of the troubadour he created sparkling prose out of thin air. Or so he thought. The engineer said we would have to do it again, and this time sing only the verses he would want on the album version. Vince said, "Just cut out the verses that don't work. This is the take I want on the album."

As I said, this was before drum machines, so the engineer rolled his eyes up in his head. He had just finished a session with Leon Russell, where the great Hal Blaine was the session drummer. He imperiously informed Vince and me that there was no way that the tempo could stay the same through twelve verses of a slow meandering folk song. Vince smiled, "Buddy's good and solid. You should be able to do it."

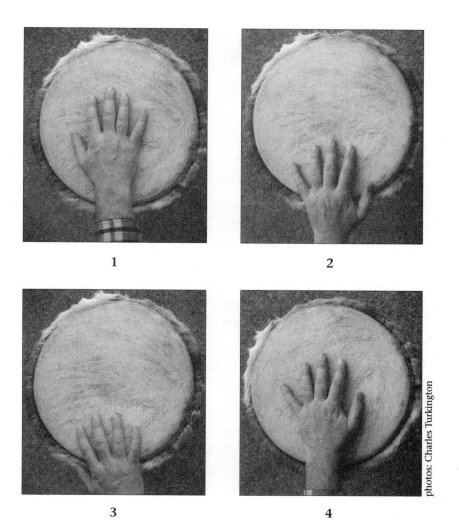

1

2

3

4

photos: Charles Turkington

Set up a steady repetitive pattern. Accent the "1" beat and the "4" beat. Repeat the pattern. Your brain will want to stop after hitting the accent on "4," but keep it going. Maintain a steady flow while hitting the accents. When you get a steady pulse going, try changing accents, then come back to the original pattern. Variation is good, but you still need to support the original groove.

The engineer sneered. "Not even Hal Blaine can do that!"

The point of this story is not that I am a better drummer than Hal Blaine. I'm not. The issue here is that rhythm, in its natural state, changes all the time. The constraints of technology changed our organic method of music into a rigid, unforgiving piece of manufactured plastic. What this does to our bodies and our minds has yet to be understood fully. The incessant banging of a drum machine has proven to be too irritating, creating a nervous, anxiety-ridden environment that is unacceptable for a pleasant listening experience. Yet, that is what is going on all day every day in our lives for simple reasons of economics.

The machinery of our lives does not have the "Quantize" button. The machines in our everyday life drive us harder and harder every day, yet we are not aware of the tempo increasing. We struggle to keep up, pay the bills, and just get by.

Keeping up is what people sometimes feel they have to do when they play in a drumming group. They have doubts about their own ability to play correctly or play enough notes. In reality, they don't have to keep up. "Give up" might be a better way to look at it, giving up all the fear that is created in imagining what you can't do. It might be better to find the downbeat and just play that. One big beat every measure. Just listen to the others who are playing and find that beginning beat and hit it. No more, No less. Let the space in between the downbeats get filled up by the other players—or better yet, by no one at all. Don't worry if it's not right. Leave that to the guys in the white lab coats. Just hit the drum and listen for the group downbeat.

8

DRUM INTIMIDATION

D on't feel intimidated by a drum, or by anyone playing a drum. It is a tool to be enjoyed and shared, and
everyone has their place in the rhythmic cosmology.
Many people feel that it is a secret that must be kept and
hoarded, but, generally speaking, people who are misers don't
really swing anyway. Feel comes from being flexible, not only
in playing but in matters of taste.

There are manners and etiquette in drumming that should
be respected. The drummers who play selfishly and don't listen to the other drummers don't have the ability to function
with equality within a group.

Performers need to support the group and not monopolize
the open spaces just for the sake of neurotic noodling. That
kind of nervous drumming is more disruptive than if the person were playing out of rhythm. This type of person doesn't
see the need for space or respect for the other drummers. There
is no need to be intimidated by such a person who is basically

unaware and uncaring of their own effect on the world. Even when they play so many notes you want to just give up, there is still no need to be intimidated by such a performer. They just have to have it explained to them.

"Back off. You're playing too much. Play softer. Leave some space, you neurotic jerk." I use some of these phrases. You can make up your own.

There are different kinds of learning in drumming. Some people learn from osmosis. They soak it up from their surroundings, even before they are born. The fetus is hearing and feeling at an early stage. Inner ear development and balance comes from reacting to rhythm and movement in the mother's womb. Rhythmically oriented babies can be born into any kind of culture. There is no racial or cultural monopoly on rhythm—what matters is what you do with what you've got. One note is enough if it's in the right spot. Brevity is still the soul of wit. The boorish players are the ones who need to prove something. They dominate, bully, and intimidate for a feeling of superiority. I try not to be hard on those types of people if they're willing to play. They can be a part of the group, but their personal psychology is where the work is needed.

What people play is what they have experienced. It's all valid. There is no need to feel intimidated because of the life you were born into, or your circumstances in playing the drum. The point is to play. At all costs, play the drum. Even if it means laughing at yourself or enjoying yourself. Even if it means allowing someone else to play something you don't understand or like. Play even if you have to learn something, or give something up to play it. Just play.

The act of hitting a drum is a great achievement for some people. They are so locked up inside their heads that the mere thought of striking a deep, resonant note on a drum is some-how outside their realm. They are the ones that need it most.

A sense of rhythm is a form of nonintellectual integration. It brings the person's attention out of their minds and into their hearts and bodies, and also into the moment. Experience is immediate in this type of drumming. No faking it by just riff-ing off and not paying attention; here every note is important. That's why the space is important. This frees the mind for a much-needed break, and gives the body something fun to do where it can be in control in a noncompetitive way.

I remember when I witnessed my first mystery on the drums. I was having my ninth birthday party and a bunch of my school friends came up to my bedroom to see my snare drum. I played a piece of written music that my teacher had given me. It was a historical drum tattoo called "Downfall of Paris." It is quite tricky. My friends all liked it, even though it was sort of academic. Then something happened that was incomprehensible to me. My fifth-grade friend, Mike, took the sticks and started playing the snare drum in a very interesting way. It was happy and syncopated, and the girls really liked it. The mystery to me was that there was no music on the music stand in front of him. He was playing without music! And the girls really liked it!

I was in a terrible state of confusion. "How can you do that?" I asked, dumbfounded.

"I just play," he said.

Since then I have been learning to just play. If I can do it, anybody can do it.

Mike was from a well-to-do family in the Midwest. They lived in a big house on a nice residential street. Funny, but on an adult return visit to the "hood," all the streets and houses seemed much smaller. I remembered Mike's family's grand piano in the living room and a coffee-table magazine that caught my eye. It was their subscription to *Downbeat,* the jazz magazine. This was an alien form of music that I didn't know anything about, but I knew that it held secrets. It was intimidating, but I came to love it, and it's still a mystery to me, even when I play it. There is a lifetime of learning in any kind of music. No one is ever fully realized or the ultimate authority. There is always something more to embrace, no matter what they tell you or try to prove on the drum or any instrument. The most advanced musicians ironically have a hard time with this subtle type of drumming. Their sense of invested work and energy takes precedence over surrendering to the group feel. They would rather stay in their technical isolation than submit to the simplicity of the group pulse. It takes a courageous musician to give up his or her technical dues and play from their heart again.

The amazing thing about rhythm is that it changes. It is a function of cultural assimilation and recycling. Popular music grows out of the rhythms of the culture. In the sixties, rock drumming evolved out of what it had been in the fifties; a certain tradition of rhythm that had evolved and become relatively simple, yet very subtle if done correctly. A little Gospel, a little hillbilly, a little Scottish jig, some Native American pounding with classical overtones and undertows. Then in the sixties, things got really interesting; Caribbean soul and Latin funk became a new and exciting ingredient. This last movement is what entered our pop consciousness at that time, along with Latin elements coming into the mainstream American culture. In terms of drumming, it consisted of a drum set being played along with conga drums. This cultural mix was actually a blending of heritages. The European grooves with Afro-Cuban and Latin. Santana, of course, comes to mind, but I had the good fortune to have worked many venues in the South, opening for the original Allman Brothers Band when Duane Allman and Barry Oakley were still alive. My band was called Bethlehem Asylum and we were a mix of everything from psychedelic R 'n B to country and jazz. After we warmed up the crowd we got to sit backstage and watch a truly great band play. The inspirational soloing that came out of Duane and Dicky and the rest of them was powered by cultural mix-masters on the drums: Jai Johnny and Butch Trucks, along with Barry Oakley on bass. There were tympani (kettle drums) on the same stage with conga drums. The mixing of cultural symbols was obvious to me. New world grooves were being born that couldn't be ignored. You could actually feel them. You *had* to feel them. The rhythm and blues grooves were sup-ported by Afro-Cuban/jazz percussion mixed with the military marching rhythms I sometimes call "Marching Through Geor-gia," which is sort of a General-Sherman-of-the-Union-Army march beat, mixed with a fat Southern swing. The rhythm sec-tion in the Allman Brothers Band is still great, and listening to Duane solo was one of the most transcendent experiences of my life. Once Charlie Dechant, our sax player, confirmed that Duane was playing the Coltrane piece "Love Supreme" on slide guitar. His Marshall amp stack was cranked up to 12. He stood at the front lip of the stage, his scuffed boot tips hanging over the edge. It was about a twenty-foot drop down to the adoring crowd. His blonde, muttonchopped face was upraised as if lis-tening to God. It was as if Duane were plugged directly into the Universe. His eyes were closed, but his ears were wide open. He leaned forward. His goldtop Les Paul hung from his

A group of jazz musicians were jamming in a Greenwich Village night club. All the players were playing a lot of notes, but the guitar player was playing only one note, over and over again. Some one asked him, "How come you're only playing one note?"

He grinned and said, "Everyone else is looking for it. I found it."

—Drummer's joke

neck like a vestment. On his left finger was a glass Coricidin bottle. It floated above the guitar neck, making sounds so beautiful I could weep and laugh at the same time. Yet all the time, he was swinging the beat so bad you had to jump up and shout. The notes Duane coaxed out were a voice, a choir, a Big

Bethlehem Asylum, 1970. Left to right: Christian, Buddy (in the polka-dot shirt), Jim, Charlie, and Danny.

Band horn section, a screaming eagle. The visions were overwhelming, but the amazing underlying power of his playing came from a combination of melody and rhythm. He could play fast notes. Faster than "Old Slow Hand" Eric Clapton, even. He could play the basic blues like it was meant to be played too, but he brought an openness to the melody with a rhythmic swing that gave it authority—more authority than if he had ripped off a thousand fast notes. He could play with rhythm and was not afraid of letting the silence come between his notes. He had no need to fill up the singing space with nervous, unnecessary notes. I still remember the power and the glory of that music.

I try to impress on people today in the drumming groups that it is possible for anyone to feel that kind of inspirational connection. You don't need muttonchops or a Marshal amp. The energy comes through with the right state of feeling. Not the size of the axe or the number of notes.

NEW RHYTHMS

The rhythms of the world are changing. The new rhythms that evolve out of our mixture of cultures will be our salvation. This will be where talking isn't needed and strangers can get along.

When we were in Bali, Indonesia, years ago, I was sitting in an obscure little shop outside of Kuta, waiting patiently while Cathy negotiated prices with the locals for some carvings we had picked out. I knew better than to negotiate myself. Cathy is an L.A.-born Filipina and could get a much better price than a big white guy like me. I was content to carry the stuff back to the jeep. I absentmindedly picked up a double-headed drum with beautifully carved dragons on it, and tapped on it while they laughed and worked on the prices. Drumming for me had been a job for so many years that I had given it up as a recreational activity, but this time I just sat there and tapped out a three-beat rhythm to help Cathy get some bidding momentum. The local guy stopped and looked at me with amazement and delight.

"You're a drummer!" he said, as if he had just discovered me.

I nodded casually, but he persisted, "No! You are really a drummer!"

I admitted that I was, as if it were some dark, hidden secret. I had long ago lost my joy in playing the drums. My straight gigs were in film production and the management would view an ex-drummer with suspicion, so I had omitted it from my resumé. What with getting screwed in the music "biz" and losing friends to drug overdoses and murders over royalties and the like, I had given up on drumming. "Yeah. I was a drummer. Big deal. Big stages. Spotlights. The whole bit. Rock star." I added cynically, looking at the smiling Balinese man. "That was a long time ago."

He shook his head.

"No! No! You are *a real drummer*!" He insisted.

I finally acquiesced. "Yeah." I mumbled. "I'm a real drummer."

He stood and waved his arms at me. *"Then play!"*

He strode out into the golden afternoon light. The huge green palm fronds filtered the sun into a yellow green glow all around us. He stood in the middle of the palm grove and called to his people. They came from different directions out of the jungle, all of them curious at his insistent tone of voice. He started to direct the activities as we set up to play. I reluctantly took the drum he handed me and sat down to play for them.

They called up a carver from the back of the thousand-year-old stone compound.

He couldn't speak English and I couldn't speak Indonesian, but we got along just fine. The fellow who just a moment before had been running the shop now donned a carved monkey mask. He explained it was made by his grandfather. It had long, hairy white eyebrows and a white moustache. He began to move with sinuous grace and slinky rhythm as we started to find our way together as drummers. The carver played a rhythm I couldn't quite get. He slowed it down and smiled.

photo: Buddy Helm

Four-hundred-year-old terraced rice paddies in Bali, Indonesia, where the author was reminded again how joyful drumming can be.

Then I showed him one I had played behind Bo Diddley many years earlier. I thought it was a pretty simple rhythm, but he scratched his head and grinned shyly just as I had a moment before. Our ears were used to hearing our own cultural rhythms. No matter how easy we thought they were, they were still foreign to someone from a different culture. The ceremonial dance the fellow in the monkey mask was performing, I learned later, was used in exorcising demons. It was an exorcism in a way for me. They showed me again how joyful drumming can be. I had been taking it entirely too seriously for too long.

They told me, "Just play!" And finally I did. We played all afternoon with some of the sweetest people I have ever met.

photo: Cathleen Javier

Native Balinese dancer emulates a monkey's movements in a ceremonial dance intended to exorcise demons.

9

THE 13 AMERICAN RUDIMENTS

The basic thirteen American drum rudiments are the backbone of American drumming. They are patterns of notes played exactly the same way every time, at a slow speed, then gradually sped up to as fast as the drummer can move their sticks, then slowed back down again, always maintaining the same "sticking" or hand sequence. This is called, "playing the rudiments open and closed."

The first rudiment I learned was called a "paradiddle." I was eight years old. The "sticking" is R-L-R-R then L-R-L-L. Saying "par-a-di-dle" evenly as you play it is the appropriate way to hear it while learning to play it. The word "paradiddle" is a Colonial American creation that may be utter nonsense, but may also be an approximation of a common drumming sound from that era. The Native American drumbeat we are the most familiar with sounds like a paradiddle. Another rudiment called the "flamacue" is also aurally taught by saying, "John-NIE-got-a-gun" when playing it, being sure to accent the second note. This rudiment may have come along later, maybe during the Civil War when "Johnnie Reb" was a real person down below the Mason-Dixon Line. This aural tradition of teaching drumming is common in various cultures. The thirteen rudiments are distinctly American.

By "distinctly American," I mean that the rhythms and rudiments are a mix of many different cultural influences that became America. The paradiddle is the Native American sound when it is played slowly, or *open*, but when the drum student learns to speed up the rudiment, or play it *closed*, the sound of that specific note pattern no longer sounds like a Pow Wow but more like a steam locomotive tearing across the prairie. Rhythms imitate the rhythms in our lives. The rhythms change as our technology and culture changes

Other rudiments, like ratamacue, flam, flamacue, five-stroke roll, lesson 25, drag, ruff, flam tap, and others, are a mix of African, Caribbean, Spanish, German, French, English, Celtic, Native American, and other cultural influences. This mixing of indigenous rhythms into the melting pot of America has resulted in a pop music that covers the world in its commonality and universal impact. Rock 'n roll did not start in the fifties in Memphis, it started at the beginning of the Revolutionary War.

Around the year 1775, the newly organized Continental Army needed drummers, just as the British Army had their drummers. Troop movement was directed by using drums. The thunder of drums was one of the few commands heard above the din of battle. The soldiers were trained to recognize these drum *tattoos* as commands for regrouping, attack, retreat, reveille, call-to-arms, and, of course, mess call. The drums were a lifeline of communications.

Q: What's a band?

A: A bunch of musicians and a drummer.

A tattoo consists of certain rudiments played in a specific order, at a brisk tempo. The tattoos evolved into songs of a sort and all the trained drummers grew up learning these different drum songs. The piece I mentioned earlier, "Downfall of Paris," is a very stirring and challenging drum piece that lasts several minutes. These pieces were also ways to compare technical abilities among competitive drummers. Many times the drummers in the thirteen colonies were young boys. The drum patterns used by the British troops were the last thing that the Revolutionary Army wanted. They needed their own drum patterns that were separate and recognizably different from the British. So, another tradition brought over from the Old World had to be discarded as a necessity of war, but later this creation of a new American style of drumming led us down the path to the distinctly American multicultural mixing of rhythms we are known for today.

The challenge then for the newly appointed American drummer was to find rhythms that stirred the soldiers to action in the face of overwhelming odds, yet kept them in a state of mind that assured that they obeyed orders. The creation of uniquely American drum rhythms came out of listening to the rhythms being played around them. The sounds came from African slaves, from the Caribbean, Indian, Spanish, as well as their primary heritage from England, Germany, France, Ireland, and Scotland. These drum patterns were taught aurally from teacher to student in a unique language developed for the sole purpose of teaching drum rudiments. This language is as unique as any technical jargon and precise, even to a fault sometimes. By this, I mean that sometimes the forest gets missed by the trees. Drummers learning by using their brains don't always evolve to the point where their body takes over, and so they play rhythms as intuitive knowledge rather than technical applications.

This intuitive feel in our rhythms is many times implied but not overtly performed. Our more savage, uninhibited style of drumming and dancing was suppressed in exchange for having a strong national beat to which we all could move, or march.

Now, this great heritage of rhythm in America is expanding outward to embrace everyone in a mix of infinite world beats. This is not so easy in our culture though. There are many folks who believe that rhythm is dangerous, or bad, or lascivious, or the tool of the devil, or worse, a tool of anarchy. Rhythm is actually one of the most sophisticated forms of organized communication ever devised, yet it can engender random and joyous behavior with just a few well-placed beats. Rhythm is a world that is full of wonderful paradoxes.

The famous painting titled "Spirit of '76" portrays two men and a young boy marching victoriously through the carnage of battle in the Revolutionary War. One is carrying a flag of the new American Republic. The oldest man is playing a fife. The fife is a small flute that for centuries in Europe has always been a partner to drums and the military. The boy is playing the large field snare drum and he is looking up with awe at the other men, or the flag, who knows. Whatever he sees is inspiring him. Or what he is playing is inspiring him. The point is that the young drummer boy plays and sees the new world and the old world. The beat carries these heroic figures along on their mission to inspire a whole country that is leaving the past and moving into the future, to the beat of the drum and the fife.

"Me and My Drum" is another story that many people remember from various Christmas collections. In the story, the young child meets God and plays his drum for him, "Par rum pa rum pum." Here the child is playing his drum directly to God, who approves, we assume. Playing a drum in adoration of the Divine has been a great tradition of drumming, a method of prayer. This has been true in all indigenous cultures, but in our technological mindset today we tend to overlook this most basic and direct form of Divine inspiration. It does seem now that people are rediscovering this basic function of the drum and getting profound results from this type of spiritual playing. This type of playing amazingly enough does not require excellent rudimentary technique or a thorough knowledge of world drum beats. All that is really needed is a desire to hit the drum and to find a steady, honest heartfelt connection to the group consciousness that is inherent when more than one person hits a drum at the same time. Keeping the downbeat nice and steady is really all the technical ability that is needed. Never mind the correct sticking.

A young Buddy performed with the Indiana "Wavettes" drum and baton unit in 1962.

10

MAGIC AND DRUMMING

ndigenous cultures the world over use rhythm to induce
trance. The drum has been a tool of ritual and magic in
many different cultures for thousands of years. The effect
of this creative visualization called magic is really separate
from the effects of the drum on the participants. In that sense,
the drum is not a tool of any one type of ritual but a versatile
instrument that can be used in many different kinds of magic
and spiritual ritual. Several ceremonial instruments are becoming popular here in the United States for drumming groups
that are striving to find a magical ritual power through the
drum. Ting Sha cymbals are from India, Tibet, and Nepal.
These small cymbals are cast in an alloy of seven metals
including silver, gold, tin, and other metals, to signify the different levels of reality in the Hindu religion. I have seen people
gently hit these small cymbals together just once and become
spellbound with the pure overtones. In India, during the celebration of the Goddess Kali, these cymbals are played at a

frantic pace, along with drums and gongs, very different from how people savor each tone here.

In India this great cacophony is overwhelming to the participant, yet there is still a pulse underneath. It is a testament to the Goddess of Chaos, who is also the Goddess of Creation. The drum used is played with sticks, giving the players great speed and volume. The gongs and cymbals and shakers are on a high frequency of confusion that befuddles the hearing of the participant, while the lower drums drive the beat at an incessant, maddening speed. The speed of the repeated pattern is faster than ritual patterns that are used in other indigenous cultures, but it is used for different reasons. The tempo of a *raga* in India is slower and more sedate, yet complex beyond the first hearing.

The Native American ritual rhythm is slower, majestic in its simplicity, and very effective in connecting the consciousness to a meditative slow cycle that emanates from the earth. In some respects the pulses of the earth and the sky and elements dictate what rhythms and at what speed the ritual drumming is performed at any given place on the planet. In that sense, we are affected by the inherent rhythmic patterns that occur in nature. We mimic them in our attempts to become more deeply connected to these elemental forces of nature. In Australia,

photo: Marcella Zinner

The author wears a bear mask during a Clearwater, Florida, drumming workshop.

photo: Buddy Helm

These New Guinea musicians play both traditional and modern instruments, mixing headhunting songs with folk tunes they learned from . . . dinner guests?

the aboriginal rhythm can resemble the loping gait of kangaroos when it is played on the *Mulga* sticks and the *Didjeridoo*.

In early Europe, when the clan or tribe was the prevailing social order, the drumming rhythms possibly resembled the animals in some way. Ponderous and heavy for a mastodon, and quicker for the deer. We mimic nature and her rhythms in all that we do.

In our technological culture the rhythms are many times completely unconscious and too rapid for detection, let alone conscious mimicking, but our subconscious strives to match the patterns anyway. The ticking of a clock has been replaced by the steady, sedate hum of cooling fans accompanying microsecond ticks of computer chips too fast for our brains to comprehend, but by which we are affected anyway on a cellular level. This complex rhythm is also influencing our behavior. We are driven by it, even to the point of panic, and we don't know why. In an attempt to be in harmony with the environment, we follow this rush toward an ideal of speed and perfection implied in the promise of the digital technological revolution. The body reacts to the imposed imperative of the time clock in some ancient survival attempt at matching the environment to the consciousness, but this results in madness.

There is no soul in the machine. We tap our finger to the tapping of the windshield wiper, we tap our foot to the busy signal on a telephone. We react to the insane beeping of a car alarm with annoyed acceptance, yet we are still deeply affected by its insistent pattern. In an earlier incarnation of our modern culture, the train was the prevailing rhythm, so prevalent it was even reflected in the songs of the day. Now, the higher RPMs of high-performance cars scream at us, insisting that we go faster and faster.

The patterns that used to be unconsciously accepted as natural and healthy: rain, thunder, wind, birds chirping, animals calling, insects clicking, and the waves lapping are now the sounds that are rare and forgotten. These sounds are even recorded and sold to those intent on recapturing a natural consciousness, but the effects of the technological culture are still more pervasive than we realize because these recordings are now digital, which means that the sound signal is broken up into microscopic intervals of sound that a computer can understand. This may sound like a natural sound, but in reality it is a fractured image with pieces too small to see, but that are still felt. Are we starting to suffer from a digital neurosis that is driving us to an even faster state of urgency?

The rhythms that we do respond to are the ones that contemporary music rhythms are based on. Reinterpreting daily rhythmic pollution is the challenge and the theme of art and music. Hence, pop music sounds like garbage trucks and jack hammers, where it used to sound like trains and planes.

Rhythm and drumming have been a constant influence on culture. In the past, drumming had been an integral part of warfare, for very practical as well as symbolic reasons. But more importantly, rhythm has affected the soldier without their understanding how or why.

Hundreds of years ago, during the Crusades, the outcome of the clash of cultures in the Holy Land was partially decided by rhythm. The European Crusaders were brave and virtuous, yet they came into the conflict ill equipped for the confrontation with the Mediterranean sense of rhythm.

The drum had, over a span of centuries, been removed from the daily lives of the Europeans. As Christianity spread, the pagan religions were wiped out. Along with this suppression, the drum, as the main tool of the pagan ritual, was also invalidated. The drum came to be seen as the tool of the devil. Previously, any individual could bang a drum and sing to the elements, to God, to nature, to the Goddess, whatever the subject. The result was a connection of great personal depth for the player. A sense of universal rhythm was what the individual needed, and by playing a drum he or she connected to the greater consciousness and shared a moment with the Divine. Christianity inserted a middle man in that direct communion with God, and that middleman deemed it necessary to remove

Q: What's the difference between a drum machine and a real drummer?

A: With a drum machine, you only have to punch in the rhythm part once.

—Internet drum joke

from the hands of the masses the most basic and simple tool for talking to God: the drum.

There were very few places a drum could be used in European celebration. It was used as part of the folk traditions, but individual drumming as prayer was mistrusted as pagan. When the best and the brightest Crusaders came to liberate the Holy Land, they encountered Saracen soldiers advancing against them, reinforced by elephants carrying huge brass tympani or kettle drums. These drums were being played with heavy, throbbing, three-beat rhythms that clouded the Crusader's minds, instilled panic, and actually threw them off balance. Meanwhile the Arab soldiers fought like men possessed; which they were. The sophisticated three-against-four rhythm put them into a deep trance that made them impervious to pain and fear. This same rhythm intimidated the Crusaders. The effect of this rhythm is unique in that it is a combination of the two basic building blocks of all rhythms; the two-beat phrase and the three-beat phrase. This particular three-against-four beat can set up an interference pattern in the listener's mind. To the inexperienced ear, these two rhythms are incompatible. They don't start and end at the same time. Like apples and oranges, they don't mix. They are irrational, in that they follow their own repeating cycles; only occasionally do they match up with the other rhythm also being played simultaneously.

The visual equivalent might be the familiar psychological image showing a black and white picture of either a vase or two faces, depending on how one looks at it. The rhythms played by the Saracens could be heard in a lot of different ways. Since the Crusaders were unfamiliar with this effect of rhythm, they feared it. The Crusaders were as frightened by the drummers as by the elephants. The clash of rhythms can actually disrupt your sense of balance.

The Europeans were willing to learn, though. They brought back the tympani drums to northern Europe and incorporated them into the music of the court and the military, and eventually into the orchestra. In the "1812 Overture" the tympani mimicking the cannons are really a distant reverberation of the Saracen drums instilling terror into the uninitiated ears of the sons of European nobility, on their quest to the Holy Land. This quest is still with us. Only now, however, we are finding that the drum is a more necessary tool for the spiritual journey than a sword.

11

THE TEMPO IS
THE THING

E ven the best of technical players can inadvertently speed up the tempo and upset the feel. The feel is not something that can be learned in the brain; it is a sensation in the body and the soul. Every pattern has an appropriate speed at which it works best, but some patterns also work well at more than one speed—depending on if it is played behind the beat or in front of the beat, or right on the beat. This beat is the constant. It is the downbeat—the big beat, the main beginning beat of a pattern. When playing a pattern, some drummers will speed the beat up until it is too fast to dance to. This results from their own inability to feel the beat, to feel their own lives. This is not a judgmental pronouncement. This is rather a condition of most people in the modern world. They are focused on getting there. On winning. On getting there with more. On being the first with the most. This anxiety tricks people into speeding up the tempos that naturally should stay constant and slow. This state of mind tricks the believer into thinking that getting there first is better. What may really be better is when everyone gets there together.

In drumming no one wins if they get to the end first. The feeling of success comes from people playing together. This is accomplished by listening to the other drummers and feeling what they are playing in relation to what you are playing. There are certain patterns that fit together at certain tempos. By not hurrying, by just listening, the different patterns fit together and everyone benefits. When the patterns are woven together by the different drummers, everyone is lifted higher, to a greater level of consciousness. This can only happen when the drummers listen to each other and monitor their own playing in relation to the others. The greater the number of drummers, the less each drummer plays. The less each drummer plays, the easier it becomes for everyone to evolve to a higher plain of awareness. The more aware the players, the more constant the tempo and the deeper the state of meditation. When the attention span of one drummer drifts away from the group, then the whole chemistry falls apart. When one drummer speeds up, the other drummers feel a fighting energy that prevents everyone from climbing up the awareness ladder together.

Humility and humbleness are critical to being a good drummer. This sense of community consciousness in a drumming group is the sense of responsibility to the downbeat. The beat is eager and willing to be played. The beat is always forgiving. Each beat is new. Each mistake is really a clue, a possibility. But drummers have a challenge: playing a rhythm and also being transported, while still paying attention to what they are playing. Soloists need not feel the temptation to show off or overwhelm the other drummers for their own ego gratification because this is a limiting factor that intimidates others. Only the most responsible and humble players can solo and still keep the feel and the pattern going at the same time. Most soloists lose the feel as soon as they start ego tripping with hot licks. A workable way to improvise in a group is to keep the theme intact while gradually adding to it, in order to evolve to a higher plane of rhythm without getting too busy. Getting too busy in the pattern jams up the flow of meditational energy through the players and dancers.

The flow of life energy can also be jammed up if the tempo speeds up. Of course, sometimes tempos do speed up, and that's okay, but many people *unconsciously* speed up the tempo. If rhythm is played at its proper tempo, the body reconnects with the sense of appropriateness in all things. If the body can feel secure in staying at a steady tempo, then a deep sense of self-confidence emerges. This self-confidence feeds out into the life of the drummer. Their actions take on authority, based on an inner connectedness to the appropriate speed of life. The sense of appropriate actions affects our life decisions in a deep and profound way. Others sense this confidence and defer to it because it is based on a truth of life, the truth of knowing where the beat is.

When a player does not know where the beat is, they panic. This panic is a sensation of being lost in the universe, of not having one's feet on the ground. As soon as they find the beat, they smile and immediately feel at home again.

Even the best drummers lose the beat. They just know how to find it again and not to panic, and they also are not hard on themselves. They forgive themselves immediately. For a microsecond they can stop playing, even in the middle of a complex solo and reestablish their own relationship to the beat. They

If you lose the beat, don't panic—there's another beat coming around again, like another bus coming by in fifteen minutes.

feel the downbeat again and they can continue with pure confidence. Many times the dancer or the listener may not even know that the master drummer has lost the beat. The master drummer does not feel chagrin at having lost the beat. He or she can laugh at it, because they know that the beat is always forgiving. The beat is willing to be played and will always be available to any drummer. If the drummer loses the beat—there is another beat coming around again, like another bus coming by in fifteen minutes. Don't panic. Just listen and feel; the beat will make itself evident and you can pick up the pattern again, fit in, and feel the beat. No reprimands. No wrong notes. No guilt. No embarrassment. Only a smile at the humorousness of the human condition. We all lose the beat, but we can find it again.

Sankola: There is no taboo in going back and getting what you forgot.

(Adinkra proverb)

12

DYING OF THIRST

A woman rolled into our shop. Tall, handsome, German, with her adolescent son. They were dressed for high-speed exercise on Montana Avenue, wearing inline rollerskates and body armor. A few of us were involved in an impromptu drumming session on a late Saturday afternoon. She timidly asked if she could enter the store on her skates and listen. I was doing my usual talking and drumming. In her skates, she towered over me—Aryan, Nordic, ice-blue eyes, and blond hair, in high-impact black plastic wrist and elbow guards. She finally admitted in unusually timid, German-accented English that she had tried to play drums many times in the past—even bought tablas to try to play. But, alas, she said that her drum teacher had told her that she could not play drums, that she had no sense of rhythm. It was obvious that she wanted to play. I told her first of all that tablas from India are some of the most challenging drums to play. They are very subtle and take quite a bit of study to even begin to feel comfortable on them. She had been trying sadly to come to terms with this expert's diagnosis that she did not have a sense of rhythm. Then she had whizzed by our store and heard drums. Not studied drums. Not drum lessons. Just people playing for fun. So she struggled up the four steps on her roller blades and came in to ask for one last chance, to just listen to the drums. She was like so many other people I have seen who are starving for rhythm in their lives. They're crawling across the desert, dying of thirst, dying for a sense of rhythm in their lives. I went into my usual beginning spiel:

"There is a big note in the middle of the drumhead. You hit it with pretty much most of your hand. On a big drum use everything; thumb, little finger, fingertips down to the heel. Don't curve your hand. Just get your hand up and let the head vibrate. The other basic note is at the edge of the drumhead, using just your fingers in a high, snapping tone. None of the notes are hit with a lot of force or tension in the hand. It's just a low note in the center and higher notes toward the edge. That's it, for now."

I hit the middle of a big standing drum and told her to do the same. She removed her wrist protectors after some coaxing. It took her a great deal of personal courage to overcome her shyness, but she did hit it. It wasn't bad for a first note. I told her to hit it again after me. She gained more confidence and some conviction and the note began to ring and have a voice of its own. I then hit the edge of the drumhead, getting a high, pinging sound. She got that one easier. I repeated the low note in the middle then the high note in a steady pattern. She played along. Low note, then high note. She became lost in the action of hitting the head and listening to the tone she was getting. She was soon playing along with me on the tall, standing African drum, smiling and moving with the beat. She even began to experiment with changing the beat; inserting a tentative note in the opening holes that she could now hear as part of the basic pattern. She took to rhythm like a duck takes to water. The smile on her face told me and the others in the store that she had broken through her assumptions and fears about herself. It had very little to do with her ability or sense of rhythm. It had the whole world to do with her own self-image.

Her main anxiety stemmed from the misbelief that she had to immediately play the most sophisticated rhythms. It takes a long time to learn some rhythms. She had been reprimanding herself for not being a great drummer before she had even become just a drummer.

Then I showed her the simplest of rhythms; two notes, one deep note in the center of the drumhead to get the vibrations going up into her body, and the high note at the edge of the head. She began to awaken her almost forgotten genetic memories of feeling a drum in her distant past. The woman as drummer, playing and healing, invoking protective earth spirits for the clan. When she did access some basic cellular consciousness with that heritage, her eyes lit up with a fire that was her life being rekindled, as if the distant past was finally coming up in her present-day consciousness and integrating her with all the women drummers of the world—past, present, and future. When she began to really play that first time, she started to nod her head with a child-like energy. It was an innocent excitement. It was a cleansing sensation for her and for all of us to see. She was shedding repressive memories just by patting the big drum on the main downbeat, then adding a few notes of her own in the open spaces.

We all have a beating heart, we all have a drummer inside of us. No need to be thirsty.

That first time she hit the drum was like opening a prison door for her. After I got her going, she took more chances and more control of her own sound. I kept a steady simple basic pattern while she took off. After a few minutes, I reluctantly brought her out of the light trance she had slid into and let her realize what she had accomplished. She had proven without a doubt that she was a drummer. She had a good sense of rhythm, but more importantly she had the desire. The techniques would come at her own speed. By telling her not to worry about all the busy fast notes of a rhythm but rather to find the big beginning beat, the downbeat, she found the path to her own drummer. She had a breakthrough in her thinking. Nothing more than that and she had become a drummer. Painlessly. Another recovering student saved from their own inner critic and from critical teachers—for the moment.

She came in for a few drumming workshops before returning to Germany with her son. She really opened up and showed to complete strangers in the group that she was actually a very good drummer underneath the conditioning she had been burdened with. She said she could actually hear the inner voices of her parents saying:

"Don't play that! You're not a drummer! Stop that right now!"

But I reminded her that she had succeeded in continuing to play the drum despite those inner voices from her childhood harassing her for things she still felt guilty about. Everyone of you can be a drummer if you can find the drummer within you. We all have a beating heart, we all have a drummer inside of us. No need to be thirsty.

13

HOLES

Some men and a few women show a nervousness about the silent spaces in between the notes when they drum. They anxiously fill up the empty space with noodling. This is in part because our body and mind need to keep some sort of inner metronome going through the silent spots in order to feel safely connected to the ongoing downbeat. Many drummers keep their foot tapping or their head nodding as their inner timekeeper. There is also the temptation to play all the possible notes, which isn't quite the right approach since it overwhelms the subtlety of any groove that has been established. In my case, people have said that it looks like I'm hitting the drum when I'm not, because my hands are keeping the rhythm going but not playing notes loud enough to be distinguishable. At other times they hear the notes but don't see my hands hitting the drum. These "grace notes" add a subtle flavor and also keep me on the groove. The real magic comes when we can let the holes in the rhythm breathe and exist on their own, on equal footing with the notes.

Some people feel anxiety about leaving silence where there could be something happening. They have been tricked into believing that the holes and spaces are to be developed, to be occupied with some human achievement—preferably their own. This is in response to avoiding the silence in those holes and avoiding their own inner silence. There is a great "kick" to the feel of a groove when an appropriate hole happens before a series of interesting notes. The silence sets up the ensuing notes so that there is a relationship between the non-notes, which is necessary for the notes to sound right. The greatest drummers don't play a lot of notes all the time, only some of the time.

The existential abyss frightens modern humans more than ever. The greatest achievement for the drummer is to allow these holes to breath. A danceable rhythm comes not from playing all the notes that are possible, but rather from leaving the right spaces. The body moves to fill those holes with movement; thus dance is born.

Modern culture tricks us into believing that holes are worthless, but just the opposite is true. The holes are actually more important than the notes being played. Without the holes, the rhythm is machine-like, unfeeling, incessant, boring, and cacophonous.

A subtle rhythm has a lot of holes and a few notes in just the right places. If a rhythm is played correctly, at the right speed, with the right holes, it is like dialing directly to the center of the Universe. Rhythms are like cosmic telephone numbers—play them right and you're talking to God. Play them at the wrong speed and nothing happens. You might get billed for a call to the wrong area code on the downside of the Universe.

The notes and the holes are also a model for the balance of the Tao, of yin and yang. It can be a model of the universe where the subtle artistic balance between chaos and coherence is demonstrated in a joyful rhythmic dance; the balance of male and female, positive and negative, good and bad, up and down. The dance of Shiva, creation and destruction, can be demonstrated in rhythm. By trusting this continuum of rhythm, we connect to the eternal rhythms and feel a sense of belonging. Even when we stop playing the rhythms, there is still rhythm pulsing along around us. This deep understanding and trust that rhythm is life, that we are drummers and dancers and can feel the movement in our bodies, gives us confidence in our everyday lives. The body is confident as well as is the mind.

When we get tricked by the culture to speed up, to fill the empty holes, to get to the end before everyone else, to play more notes than are necessary, we lose the beat. We then lose the organic connection to our correct responses to life. Our intuitive improvisational decisions are then made out of fear, not out of confidence and joy.

The earth is in need of more drummers. The vibration emanating from hand on skin is essential to the integration of the planet. It is a nonintellectual wisdom and it is available to all of us. It is as easy as dialing a phone number to God, but this can happen only when the right holes are respected as well as the right notes.

photo: Wriston Jones

Buddy teaching a workshop at the Roswell, Georgia, Women's Center.

14

PATHFINDER

Many people equate drumming with violence. This assumption is usually based on the appearance of force being exerted by the macho kind of drummers. In reality, muscle and force can be deterrents to good drumming. Relaxed drumming is the only way that the fast patterns can be played, especially for any extended length of time. Otherwise, we burn up our energy reserves too soon. Our inner critic habitually tenses our muscles when we try to play fast. It is a holdover from the fight-or-flight reactions triggered when we are in a survival situation. Getting tense and forcing our hands and arms to perform faster and harder only prevents real flowing rhythms from happening. It actually slows us down.

The brain is an amazingly complex computer and learning machine. When first learning a drum rhythm, the inner critic is actively monitoring the student's hand movements and comparing that to the sounds that the inner critic thinks are correct. This kind of control is a survival mechanism that applies to more critical situations than playing drums. Nevertheless, our inner critic is functioning—listening, evaluating, and making suggestions—or rather pronouncements. These pronouncements are sometimes even condemnations. There is that inner voice saying: "You're doing it wrong!" "You're not supposed to do that!" "Stop!" "You're not a drummer!"

This self-monitoring process slows down any fast playing. It's important to a certain extent for learning, but after the basic lesson has been absorbed, students need to let the knowledge move into their bodies, let it go out of their brains and down into their hands and arms and body where it can be used quickly. The nerve synapses don't need to be relayed all the way back to the brain for approval. There is innate wisdom in the body that can make these microsecond decisions without the inclusion of the brain.

The inner critic does not give up so easily, though. When the speed of a pattern increases, the inner critic tries to process the increase in information. That's its job. The student becomes anxious, "Oh no! It's too difficult for me to do! I'm too stupid to do this. I have no sense of rhythm. I'll give up and go get a day job."

This frustration is temporary. Players should take a big breath and let it out, forgive themselves, and give themselves permission to move forward into uncharted territory, also to let the inner critic take a much-needed vacation. When this happens, the playing suddenly becomes effortless. The sensation that we are "riding the beat" takes over. We lose track of time and place and become totally absorbed in the sound and rhythm. What was impossible a moment ago now becomes like second nature. The brain learns to take a backseat to the overall process that happens more in the body than the brain. Take a breath and let go; just keep on playing.

Another function of this inner critic and its survival mechanisms is muscle tension. The inner critic mistakenly thinks that tensing the muscles is a good idea. Invariably it will slow you down, and in some cases even injure you. This is obvious in martial arts. The immortal Bruce Lee was the Balanchine of fighting. He was as supple as a cat and always smiling, even laughing—not out of cynicism, but out of fun. He was relaxed and in a lighthearted state of mind, even in combat.

This is where force and drumming might get confused. In Aikido, for example, the opponent's force is used to deflect or defeat them. The aggressor is the one exerting and upsetting the balance that aikido can use as a weapon in defense. In drumming there is a different and much more subtle allowance of energy flow.

One dark night I was taken to his private academy to meet a very famous martial arts teacher. I was shown into the large padded studio, joining a small crowd of international spectators while this man demonstrated various knife fighting techniques to a group of high-degree black belt students. On the walls were portraits of the different masters he had studied with and taught, both women and men, from various countries including China, and from his home in the Philippines. He was as fluid as a dancer and as assured as any master could hope to be in their art form. When he saw that one of his students had brought me to meet him, he bowed off the mat and all the students bowed deeply in reply. These students were men from various enforcement agencies, police forces, and Special Forces. They all treated him with the utmost respect. I prepared to bow to him as he approached me, but he caught me off guard by bowing first very deeply in front of me, in front of this august group of fighters.

The group of people standing around me all stepped back and took a look at me with bewilderment and sudden respect. A few bowed slightly out of deference to their master's show of respect to me. I got a funny rush as they looked at me, thinking, "Who is this bad dude?"

Then it made sense to me. He was appointing me his personal instructor. He was a master, even as a student. I felt compelled to teach him whatever he wanted to know about drumming within my very humble abilities. Nonetheless, it was a very cool moment.

He didn't call himself a master, although everyone else did. He referred to himself as a student for life. He teaches across the country and around the world. He explained later that he wanted to play drums in his classes, to instill in his students a flow that he knew they needed but he himself could not intellectually learn. When I began to work with him on an individual basis, I came to realize that he was intent on learning everything I could teach him. He would come promptly every week to his morning lesson, no matter if he had been in Copenhagen or Princeton or Tokyo the day before. He would admit that he had practiced over and over again the same pattern that I had shown him the week before, but then it would change on him and he couldn't get back to the original pattern. He was sad and frustrated. I congratulated him. His drumming was alive. It was changing. All he had to do was to follow it. This confused him, because he thought that this business of drumming was a set process, with specified hand positions and exact hand movements, the same every time—which it can be—but that is so boring. It is dead drumming. He approached it with rigidity, preventing him from going as fast as he needed to play. This was really ironic because he was faster than anyone when it came to hitting, kicking, or stick fighting, but I wanted him to play fast and loose at the same time. His hands could not go as fast as mine, which was bewildering to him. He knew more martial arts than possibly any person alive, and had been Bruce Lee's partner for many years (he is featured in some Bruce Lee movies with dazzling effect), yet he was sweating profusely after playing drums for an hour, and I was just as relaxed as when we started.

"You really have to be in shape to do this!" he exclaimed, which was really funny because he was in much better shape than I could ever hope to be, even though he was older than me.

"You have to be relaxed." I answered. "Let your hands and arms do what they know how to do."

His eyes lit up. "Bruce Lee said the same thing to me!" he exclaimed. "He told me that I was 'intellectually bound.'"

I tended to agree with this prognosis. It is the state of mind for most of us. Then he stated with conviction, "You are the Bruce Lee of drumming!"

"That's very nice of you to say that, Dan. But what's happening here is that you are coming to me to hear the same things that Bruce told you ten years ago. I appreciate the compliment anyway. Even if it's not true."

Bruce Lee was the Cha-Cha champion of Hong Kong. This really impressed me. Bruce Lee always seemed to be having fun, even when he was fighting. It all seemed like a dance to him. He had the overview that kept him relaxed, which meant that he could go as fast as need be. As Dan frowned and sweated at the tasks I was putting in front of him, I finally stopped him and said, "Dan, you are playing everything correctly, but you are doing it wrong." He frowned, full of desire to understand; the eternally perfect student. "What am I doing wrong?" the master asked.

"You're not smiling." I said. "You ought to be enjoying this." I could see the light go on in his head. He got it. He actually let himself smile.

In the end he did become what I wanted him to become, but it may not have been what he had intended. He became a "Fearless Improvisor"—willing to take chances and not let his own fear stop him from experimenting with rhythm. This meant that his sense of rhythm was alive and changing. He could make up moves on the drum that would feel appropriate. He could play a basic pattern, then change it, add his own creative notes, then fall back into the basic pattern again, always keeping the basic downbeat nice and steady. Some of his martial arts students were drummers. One man is Puerto Rican and a truly great drummer. Dan had innocently said after one of his advanced martial arts classes that he too was playing the drums. His student wanted to hear what Dan had learned and was somewhat critical of it. Dan's playing was humble compared to the man from Puerto Rico, where drumming is like a national religion. Dan showed off his simple patterns, then Dan's student showed him some pretty hot stuff. When he told me the story I reminded Dan to not be intimidated by this hot drummer's fast hot licks. The point is to feel the groove. The beginners can play along with the advanced if you remember this. Stay on the downbeat, follow the groove, and enjoy it. This is much easier than trying to learn kung fu. And it doesn't hurt as much either.

"Treat the drum like a woman," said Tito Puente's conga player.

"Don't hit it. Caress it. Make it sing. Treat it like a woman."

I think the term "Fearless Improvisor" can apply to someone who plays from conviction, trust, and self-confidence, no matter how good they are in relation to the rest of the world.

Once Dan began to take chances and play something different than what I showed him, he began to relax and have fun. He was finally stepping out of the intellectual restrictions that Bruce Lee had observed in him many years earlier. Dan actually seemed to be enjoying himself while he played, which was all I could hope for as his drum coach.

There is a confusion of identities about a drummer being a "warrior." This is macho bullshit. This attitude of the warrior drummer can create a dead end in a drummer's development because it is based on the wrong assumption that the drummer can exert power and control over the rhythm. It is the rhythm that carries the power. Not the player. The player is a servant. This quotation is from an African drummer; "I do not come to deliver a slave into bondage, I come to play for the dance," sums it up nicely.

The ability to surrender to the rhythm is a quality that has been lost in our technological culture. Control has become an obsession.

Surrendering is not a complete surrender, though. It is not all or nothing. A matter of degree is needed. In hitting a drumhead for the first time, people will first assume that their hand must be rigid. This creates a flat thin sound, not a deep resonant drum note. I suggest that they relax their hand, then hit it again. Then they invariably let all tension drop from their hand and slap the head with all the effect of a wet rag. The solution is somewhere in between. A balance of just the right amount of tension in the hand and wrist to create a striking implement, but not too much tension that would prevent flexibility and speed. This also changes with each beat. Sometimes the hand will flex, sometimes it will relax. The striking of the head is more of a purposeful caress. This also allows drummers to play for long periods of time without hurting themselves.

The tendency for an intellectual to assume that an extreme decision is the answer in any given situation is a typical techno-culture habit. The beauty of drumming is that there is always moderation. There is moderation in striking the head with varying amounts of force, also there is moderation in the amount of attention from the brain in watching over the playing. Finally, there is moderation in the numbers of notes. "Less is more better."

In setting up a pattern with a group of players, the trick to remember is that there is always room for more holes. There is never enough room for more notes. Playing in a group sometimes resembles real estate developers rushing in to exploit a pristine piece of swampland in hopes of making profit and glory instead of respecting this primordial connection to our past. The real challenge is to feel the spaces between the notes and let them live. That is where the feel really is. The notes only let us know where the holes are. This respect for the open spaces is a lost ability, partly because of the warrior mentality that has pervaded so many cultures. Warriors need to fill space with their own energy in order to feel needed. To let the holes live is to surrender to the greater whole. The individual loses some sense of their own importance when that happens. When this humility is achieved, there is a massive breakthrough of consciousness in all those sharing the rhythmic experience. There is transcendence of the daily grind into a larger, wider state of understanding. There is happiness, a sense of connectedness to all living things, an acceptance of one's place in the scheme of things. Belonging to the whole is not always the way warriors think.

There is also another illusion—that the warrior is seduced by: the idea that drumming gives them power. Power corrupts. In drumming you are given a gift of the power as it passes through the drum and through you. It is not yours to keep. It is going somewhere else.

All this debunking of the warrior ethic creates a dearth of purpose for those of us who think being a warrior is the only useful self-identity. Other mythical identities are just as useful here. One of these might be called "the pathfinder."

The pathfinder is a man or woman who is courageous, adventurous, re-sourceful, yet sensitive to the environment, seeking knowledge of the new terrain but not defacing it or stealing from it. The pathfinder returns to his or her tribe and relates to them qualities of the terra incognita so that the next generation of seekers can find the new land for themselves. The pathfinder does not control, or defeat, yet there is great opportunity for challenge, personal growth and achievement, and sense of self-worth—all this without subjugating the indigenous culture,

photo by Charles Turkington

The trick is to stay on the downbeat, follow the groove, and enjoy.

clear-cutting the terrain, or raping and pillaging. The pathfinder does not supplant the warrior though. That won't happen until there is no need for war.

15

WISTFUL

An older woman friend came to one of our drumming workshops and mentioned that she had attended a beginning drumming class at a local African drumming school. She said that the instructor was very good, but that he was wistful when trying to teach the beginning students. I asked her what she meant by "wistful" and she explained that this respected African drummer and teacher at one point just sighed, and said:

"I just *wish* that you could feel the power of the rhythm!"

She said that she would rather that he just play instead of being so forlorn about the problems of the beginners.

A light went on in my head. I realized that he was having a hard time in bringing the beginners to an understanding of basic rhythm. I was from the same mindset as the beginners, and he was from an entirely different mindset. He may not be able to put the basics of rhythm into the vocabulary of our technological mind. In a sense I understand that what I am doing is missionary work to my own people. I come from a technological mind and I have to some extent learned to be intuitive in the drumming. He had grown up in a culture where drumming was as common as eating and sleeping. He had learned to drum while still in his mother's belly. I had learned using my mind, then slowly over the years, I had come out of my mind and into my body to play the drums.

His students were intent on playing the drums. Too intent. Their brains were too eager. They would speed up after playing the pattern through just once; they couldn't just relax and stay at the same speed. Their intellects were eagerly engaged, focusing on labels instead of hearing and feeling the movement of the rhythm. They were trying to memorize proper beats rather than just play. They weren't letting their bodies learn the beats. The students were in their brains and not in their bodies. This method of rote repetition seems to put the spirit to sleep in the student. This is a result of cultural conditioning. They were approaching drumming as an intellectual challenge; i.e., "If I hurry up and learn this drumming thing, then I will be a better person."

People can't learn to swim if they don't know they're in the water.

I was having some success by letting people discover their own sense of rhythm through letting go of their intellectual minds and getting into the feel, getting into how their bodies were reacting to the rhythm.

Such a basic assumption by, for instance, an African master drummer that his students could already feel was based on his own cultural richness. The beginning students were locked up in their brains and not willing to let their bodies play. Maybe he didn't realize that not only were his students born into a rhythmic desert, they were also tricked into believing that they were in a Garden of Eden and everyone else in the world was deprived. He had been born into a rhythmic garden and could not understand how distant these other people were from his own lush natural experience.

This phenomenon is common among indigenous peoples when they try to understand the technological mindset. The body/mind separation in the civilized person is deeply ingrained. The primitive mindset of indigenous people can't comprehend the scope of this disability that we in the technological world are struggling with. The use of words like primitive is just for the sake of explanation and has no bearing on reality, by the way.

Another example comes to mind: an obviously bright, healthy WASP male who creates computer systems also trades African rhythms on the internet with other drummers, but this fellow cannot participate in a drumming group with drummers who want to just play. He is so concerned with the correct notes that he stops the whole group if someone is not playing what he considers to be the correct authentic African beat. I do not criticize the desire for accuracy, but I do pity those poor souls who do not allow themselves permission to swing.

photo: Marcy Zinner

Buddy teaching a workshop at the Metaphysical College and Church in Clearwater, Florida. He plays the tambourine with his foot, maintaining the downbeat so no one gets lost.

16

RHYTHMICALLY CHALLENGED

Drumming seems to be a mystery to many people. Some are afraid of drums and of rhythm. It's evident in their lives and in their relationships with other people and with the environment. This is not to say that these rhythmically challenged people are sick or at a disadvantage, because in actuality most of us are in this category to a lesser or greater degree.

Over and over again I've witnessed a moment of breakthrough when a person stops reprimanding themselves and starts to just play. Usually it's not a complicated pattern; maybe they manage to play just the downbeat with a little extra note for added flavor but the amount of healing energy that is released in that person is always amazing and rewarding. It is also very contagious and everyone in the group benefits.

When we can get past our inner critic and begin to feel rhythm and play along, something changes in our brain chemistry. Circuitry in the brain is rerouted and new muscle neuron pathways are awakened—some for the first time.

I encourage people not to become frustrated if they are not getting a rhythmic pattern. The inner critic is doing its best to interfere. That is its job. As a survival mechanism, the inner critic checks all the available stimulus inputs; ears, hands, eyes, feet, etc., and decides if the performance is up to its standards. Ironically, the inner critic thinks that it is usually hearing well enough, meaning that it hasn't come to the realization that it is not hearing all of the subtle elements of rhythm. This is a humbling experience for the control freak that is our inner critic. When the inner critic learns to differentiate more precisely, then we begin to grow as drummers. It has less to do with talent than with the willingness to listen.

In learning to play a drum, the inner critic is checking the hands in relation to what it thinks the hands should be playing. That judgment is based on what the lesson has been, or what the cultural bias has been, or any number of other irrelevant issues.

When the inner critic is happy, it is managing all of this inflow of information. When the inflow becomes too much, the inner critic sends out messages like; "Too much info!" or "You're not capable of doing any more, because *I'm* not capable of processing any more!" The truth is that you as a drummer are capable of doing much more than the inner critic is capable of processing. Subtle rhythmic decisions can no longer be made by the brain. The quick movements must be relegated to the hands where the decisions can be made immediately. Going back to the brain to get an okay for the next movement is akin to waiting for the Federal government to send you permission to walk across the street.

But the impression that the beginning drummer gets is that he or she is not getting it, that they are dumb, or clumsy, or not capable of playing. That is actually a good sign. Give yourself a break, take a deep breath, let go of the frustration, forgive yourself, and above all keep playing. Eventually you will be doing what you were told you could not do. The inner critic has to just give up. That will happen over and over again. Each time, the inner critic must be released from its self-imposed job of being in control. This then lets the body do what it knows it can do on its own.

This change in attitude is profound to witness. I've seen people even cry when they begin to feel a sense of rhythm come into their bodies for the first time.

To tell the truth, I don't know all the ramifications or repercussions from this type of drumming, but I do know that there is joy in the person when they get to this point of giving themselves permission to play a drum.

Rhythmically challenged people think that they are expected to play a lot of notes in order to be a drummer. The opposite is true. Less is definitely better. If, for example, we play only the downbeat, we can feel the basic pulse. This requires no more performance than hitting the drum at the beginning of each repeated pattern on the downbeat.

Another challenge for intellectually oriented people is to listen and not become bored. Listening is a group activity. Listening to others play while you also play is a humbling and a learning experience. What we have not stressed in this culture is ear and hand coordination. We have plenty of eye-hand training, but very little ear-hand training. Listening to what someone else is playing and then fitting what you play into what they are playing is the first step in becoming a group drummer. This is not accomplished by insisting that everyone is less important than you are. The challenge is to identify the downbeat in whatever pattern is going on. The downbeat is the cornerstone. It's what rhythm is built on.

The phenomenon of feeling rhythm in your body and your mind creates a state of being that ideally can be transcendental. This state of bliss is a tempting pitfall for beginning and advanced drummers alike. The body responds to a drum pattern by aligning itself in some way to the rhythm being played. The body's metabolism gets in sync with the pattern. This is sometimes called "entrainment," and can happen with either slow or fast tempos. But what happens to the mind when this occurs is even more unusual. The brain slides quite easily into a trance state. sometimes called the alpha state. Whatever it's called, the essential element of this state of being is that the mind escapes its own intellectual fetters and journeys off on its own. It is released from its survival program, and trips out. The challenge for the drummer is to keep part of their conscious mind in touch with the other drummers and the rhythms that are being played. Otherwise, each drummer goes off in their own direction, rhythms fall apart, and the result is confusion.

The breaking up of attention is actually a useful result of drumming. Your attention span becomes divided into parcels that rotate around your body while you are playing. Some attention is on the downbeat, some attention is on your right hand, some attention is on your left hand, some on your mouth if you are speaking or singing. Attention is something that can be subdivided, but the thing to remember is to not panic when your attention starts to wander. It is investigating other areas that may need some attention. You will want to remember to always keep moving your attention. Letting it settle on one spot, say your left hand, or what to eat for lunch, leaves you unconnected to the downbeat of the group, and if you lose touch with the downbeat, you no longer are riding the groove, and the group consciousness falls apart.

One of the hardest things for people to deal with is getting bored. "Must I play the same old part?" This is one of the hardest things to understand. Constancy is one of the rarest elements in our culture.

The illusion that you are playing the some old thing over and over again comes from not listening to what you are really doing. Boredom comes sometimes from assuming that you are doing the right thing, but in reality, when you think you are doing the right thing, you are actually losing touch with the right thing. There is a subtle variation even when you play exactly the same part. This is because we are human and cannot play the exact same thing every time. There are slight variations within the pattern in relation to the groove and the downbeat. This subtle variation is what gives the feel to the pattern. If we can pay attention to how each beat and pattern relates to the overall groove, then we suddenly perceive that every note is a new note. Every pattern is a newly born pattern in relation to the underlying groove. This sense of discovery is what can keep the process interesting. It involves quite a bit of listening, though. This doesn't happen if someone assumes that they are playing the right part. Or that it is good enough. Or that they are too good to be playing a simple part.

This self-centeredness comes partly from the way our cultural attitudes are set up. The rush to do more, to accumulate more, to buy more, to go faster, to get there first, to win, creates an isolated personality. Drumming is one way for total

By keeping time, we are released from time.

strangers to participate together that gets them all in touch with the moment. This sensation of being primarily in the moment is what gives us this sense of relief and joy and cooperation.

By staying in touch with the present moment, the subtleties of each note become interesting. In India whole pieces of music are created to investigate the subtle relationships between two notes that are right next to each other on the musical scale. To our uneducated ears, this may sound monotonous, but the subtleties that exist in that relationship are as immense as the universe. Our inability to understand or appreciate that small universe diminishes our own world.

Staying in the moment is very hard for modern culture. The temptation is for us to whizz off to the next flash, the next blaze of glory, the next special effect. This headlong rush into the future leaves a mess in the past. No one is aware of the garbage they leave behind them when all they see is the glitz of the next big thing.

Paying attention to the moment in drumming serves another purpose too. It frees the players from the constraints of time. After playing for a while, people stop and smile, and some one inevitably wonders, "How long have we been playing?" Usually, its hard to tell exactly how long we've been playing. By keeping time, we are released from time.

17

COMPETITION

I came across a picture of me in uniform; I was tall and almost handsome, and I had a chestfull of drumming medals. I was fourteen years old, six feet tall, no major pimples, a flattop, and a big grin. The world was my oyster.

Competition in drumming came in various shapes and sizes. Starting at the age of nine I would assiduously study a piece of drumming music for months, performing it each week for my drumming teacher, then competition time would arrive and with sweaty palms I would perform my prepared pieces in front of a panel of stern judges, in turn with hundreds of other children. The events were citywide, regional, and state competitions. The medal for drumming excellence had a red, white, and blue ribbon at the top with a brass, silver, or gold medallion hanging from it, in the shape of Indiana. Engraved on the state of Indiana were the different designations: Solo, Duet, or Ensemble. Drumming ensembles were great events of technology and precision, as well as amazing percussion events. The race was on for new drumming technology in Elkhart, Indiana in the early sixties. All the musical instrument manufacturers had factories there. I walked by Conn and Selmer every day on my way to junior high school.

Inside these clean factories were the craftsmen who made band instruments for the world. Selmer saxophones are like the Stradivarius of brass reed instruments. Bundy clarinets, George Way drums, Ludwig drums, the list of makers was long. I walked by these factories on my way to junior high school and listened to the saxophone testers trying to get the high, difficult accidental notes that were the trademarks of the great jazz innovators of the forties, fifties, and sixties: Coltrane, Charlie Parker, Ornette Coleman. I heard it everyday. It poured out of the factory windows and onto the streets. It was a strange juxtaposition of New York City onto the Midwest.

I marched each weekend with several different drum corps. These were not the militaristic V.F.W. type of drum and bugle corps; we were part of the National Baton Twirling Association. Competition was tough, but our outfits were entertaining. Our Senior Corp uniforms were black-sequined, flat-brimmed flamenco hats (with dingle balls that drove me nuts when I was playing the huge bass drum), and a red sequined cummerbund and vest that grew heavier as we marched. Sometimes the parades were five miles long.

After I became an adult, my chiropractor could not figure out why my upper back had such odd subluxations. The bass drum harness I had worn for years as a preteen had taken its toll. I also wore a kilt in a Scottish bagpipe and drum corps. We competed in parades, open fields, and cavernous auditoriums, taking top honors at national competitions. The corps were comprised of twenty to thirty girls and a dozen or so boys. We were driven to the competitions in buses and were strictly supervised. We stayed in hotels with the other corps at the national competitions. In the years of the civil rights demonstrations, around 1962, national competition was held in Jackson, Mississippi. We rode down there in two large chartered buses and were almost mistaken for Freedom Riders coming down from "Up North." The Freedom Riders were groups of Northern social activists who were agitating for equal rights for Blacks in the Deep South. The locals mistrusted any Yankees coming down, fearing they would stir up trouble. It was dangerous.

We were generally unaware of that type of problem because we were insulated in more ways than one. The boy drummers spent most of their time with the girl baton twirlers, showing off on their big, deep, field snare drums. That's a heavy drum with shiny tuning bolts. The sound projected across a football field and could be heard distinctly enough for fifty pairs of feet to march in unison. It was raw drumming power.

When we traveled on buses we checked out the other sex with naive curiosity. At my age, I had yet to hit

Buddy, at fourteen, marching in a drum competition.

the hormone rush. We were still working on hand and wrist technique on the drums.

My own drum and baton corps was called the Wavettes, after a wonderfully motivated woman named Wava who organized the groups. Our national nemesis was Miller's Blackhawks from Dayton, Ohio, who were national champions for years. They dressed in black leather. The drum section was very good, but they weren't as good as ours. We took first place as a drumming section, but as a whole corps we couldn't compete visually with our sequins and dingle balls. The music was great. We played the bolero, "Carmen," with three snare drummers, two tenor drummers, one bass drummer, percussion, and a twirling cymbal player, along with a conglomeration of glockenspiel bells and bugles, while thirty-two girls twirled their batons and marched the bolero. It was wholesome, clean fun.

But when the Blackhawks marched out onto the arena floor to the somber clicks of their snare drummers hitting only the shiny chrome rims, the tension in the room tripled. Then suddenly the line of eight field snare drums exploded into the most aggressive military rudimental showmanship imaginable, while the girls strutted and maneuvered. I lusted after them. I couldn't help it. All the color guard girls had straps across their chests and short skirts and shining, knee-high leather boots. Their drummers were excellent, although our drum section was better, but their overall show was overwhelming. The Blackhawks always won first place as the best NBTA corps in America. They were hot.

Many years later, I was visiting San Francisco for the first time. It was about 1971. By sheer coincidence, the annual competition of the National Baton Twirling Association of my childhood was being held at precisely the time I was walking by the downtown auditorium. I noticed the banner outside and strolled in at exactly the same moment that the Miller's Blackhawks were entering the competition arena; somber, rigid, stern. Marching to the terse clicking of sixteen snare drum sticks hitting the polished chrome rims in unison. Then, just like nine years earlier, the eight snare drums, two bass drums, cymbal players, four tenor drummers, and a regiment of bugles launched into their routine with the bone rattling power of total authority. They had been world champions for the whole time I had been out learning how to just play. It was as if I had stepped back in time to my preadolescent childhood. The Blackhawks hadn't lost a bit of their polish and aggressive flair. They also still held the national top honors. I couldn't believe it. At least nine years had passed and I still lusted after them. I also couldn't believe that my timing had been so exactly correct that I had seen them. There is most definitely a sense of timing in the Universe, although sometimes it can have a bizarre sense of humor.

These days, drumming competition can get even more archetypal than that, as well as more personal. Many women are afraid that the domain of drums belongs only to men. Many men feel this way too. In reality women and drumming have a great ancient tradition, and in my drumming corps, I played alongside the daughter of my drum teacher, who was also a woman. I also played with women drummers in school.

Certain types of competitive intimidation come from drummers who are needy. They need approval from drumming. They treat it as an exclusive club in order to feel superior. They have inadequacy anxiety so they play the drums. They are nervous drummers. They are worried about other people's mistakes. They have very personal reasons to play the drums, and they can make it difficult for others to enjoy drumming.

There is also cultural competition and intimidation. I didn't play with anyone but White boys like myself until my family moved to the Deep South. Florida and Georgia became my home at the still impressionable age of thirteen. I was suddenly cut off from the world of classical music, but I was blessed with having been given a solid background in music theory. Mrs. Trafford, my drum teacher back up in Elkhart, also gave me an open mind toward all kinds of music.

Rhythm belongs to the world. Nobody owns it.

Arriving in the swampland of central Florida, I looked around me and grew bitter. There weren't any drum teachers who could take me further in my classical musical education. I could sight-read music well enough to get into the Marine Corps band at the age of fourteen, but I couldn't really swing well enough to play with a local country and western group. That soon changed though. I realized that rhythm belonged to the world. It came from the world. It wasn't any one culture's domain or property. Nobody owned it. Then I really began to hear rhythm and blues, soul music, rock 'n roll, country, Afro Cuban, country blues, shuffles, jump boogies, ska, swing, chanka-chanka, Caribbean, reggae, Gospel, folk music, New Orleans "Second Line," the list goes on to infinity. There were an infinite number of rhythms around me, all being played by people who weren't as trained as I was.

All of these rhythms do something to us. I was lucky enough to get the inspiration from all the different kinds of musicians, whether they could read music or not and whatever culture or race they were from. I was exposed also to a certain amount of bigotry from different sides. Of course there was the white racist type, but there was also bigotry from people who didn't think I could play certain kinds of music because I was a White boy from the Midwest. This may be true to a certain extent, but the love of the music for me was the motivation and I learned as much as I was able to absorb about the basics of the rhythms.

"You funky fo' a white boy," was a refrain I heard quite a bit. A lot of what rhythm is about is about the culture that it comes from; the food, the lifestyles, the mores, the art, and religion. This gave me a way to understand different people and their cultures, not in an intellectual way but from a feeling approach. The sense of elitism that certain musicians had about their pure forms of music didn't deter me. I wanted to know and understand and to even play their music to some extent. I had nothing to prove. I just wanted to play.

Recently, a woman who is a professional dancer came to our drumming workshop and told me that she was getting drumming lessons from a drummer she had been working with. There was a lot of philosophizing from the guy about his heritage and the drum. She said he went on about its spiritual place in the cosmos and in his culture. This is important, but she felt that it was getting in the way of her learning to play. She felt intimidated by his dogma, by his judgmental attitude. Heritage is fine, but if it gets in the way of the student learning to enjoy playing then what's the point?

Getting ourselves free of the constraints of pride leads to a greater ability to groove, no matter what race or culture we're from. Drumming is at its best when everyone looses their individual sense of race preciousness and for a short time we can see ourselves as a functioning member of a whole group. Amazing cooperation!

For anyone posing as a teacher to instill in the student any sense of shame or of being less than able to learn because of their cultural or racial background is to make it worse for everybody. Hidden agendas and power plays are part of drumming and I try not to pay much attention to them.

Competition is also a part of drumming, but I've come to believe that it comes mostly from an overabundance of testosterone rather than from the act of drumming.

18

HOPE FOR THE RHYTHMICALLY CHALLENGED

I've discovered that people learn in different ways. They use their brains and bodies in different ways to learn drumming patterns.

The woman dancer who came into our workshop had been learning to play congas from a very excellent Puerto Rican drummer, even though she was intimidated by him. She persisted in listening to him and working out the conga drum pattern that he had shown her. She had difficulty in keeping the pattern going at a steady rate. She was so caught up in getting the hand sequence correct that she forgot the most important part of playing a drum: the downbeat. She was so inside herself that she didn't realize that the downbeat was something to be shared with the world and with other drummers. She was also entirely in her own head and not in her body. The feel was not there. She was caught up with getting the lesson correct.

Now, this teacher is a very good drummer, but he might have emphasized things in the same way that he had learned to play. That's all well and good, but in this woman's case, she was missing the groove for all the notes she was trying to play. When she showed up at one of our drumming workshops, I asked her to just play something much simpler than what her teacher had shown her, and also to play along with everybody else, keeping in mind that the downbeat was the most important thing to listen for. Not the individual notes, not the hot little syncopated licks that her teacher had played, but just the downbeat. At the beginning of each repeated pattern I looked at her and nodded on the downbeat. She began to relax and to feel. Gradually she was learning rhythm in a different way than she had been learning with her teacher. I gave her a gourd shaker, showed her how to hold it, and how it could be easily played. I also mentioned that the shaker rhythm is underneath all other more sophisticated rhythms. It is like the breath or the heartbeat to a pattern. It's always there, in the background, underneath all the flashy soloing, and it is very important because it is like glue for all the other percussionists. When it is played correctly, the group really swings. She took the gourd and began to experiment. The rest of the drumming group proceeded to work on some simple pattern that I had thrown out for us to try. She closed her eyes and became lost in listening and feeling the shaker. As we played, we all forgot about her predicament. Suddenly, she got it. The pattern she found in the shaker locked right in to what we were playing and everyone looked at her and smiled as we grooved along. Her eyes were shut and she was smiling. When she opened her eyes and realized that she had become part of the group, she shared that smile with all of us. After that she went back to the conga drum and began to find the same feeling on that drum. Soon she was inserting some pretty interesting licks into the pattern that we were maintaining. She wasn't showing off, she was experimenting. She then fell back into the basic pattern and supported the groove while others tried in their own way to journey outward from the basic pattern. We all laughed after we finished because everyone knew exactly the moment when she stopped using her brain and began to use her whole body to play. It didn't matter if the pattern was correct. We all knew that it was right.

This distinction between learning to play with our brain rather than learning to play with our whole body is a great stumbling block for many of us, because once we get locked up in our brains, trying to figure out how to play the correct part, we lose contact with the common downbeat and we cease to feel the groove. This is a very abstract idea, an example of why music is so elusive when it is being taught. The brain is needed to understand the theoretical notes, but the brain is not needed to play them. The brain gets in the way. It is more concerned with correctness of technique than it is with feel, because feel does not reside in the brain. The great irony for many sincere drumming students is that they never get past the first hurdle of leaving their intellect behind and getting to the good part, which is nonintellectual. We are always facing this problem in our lives. The illusion that our brains will save us from any dilemma that confronts us gets us into more trouble.

The process of knowing the difference between feeling and thinking is what we get familiar with. When we begin to drum from our hearts, this feeling of not thinking is a new and fascinating sensation and it continues to be fascinating even as we become more adept at playing drums. That state of mind that

When we accept the state of nonmind, we can better use our intellect for what it was intended.

lets the intellect take a vacation is a paradox. It's quite funny when we try to articulate that state of being. The breakthroughs that I have witnessed in beginning drummers are something that they take with them out into the world and use in their lives. It is not just about drumming. It is about getting out of prison, the prison of our rational brains. This is not to say that we leave the rational behind and float off into anarchy. Just the opposite. It gives us a more complete organizational model to work with; something that exists outside the rational, cause-and-effect reasons for living. When we know and accept this state of nonmind, then we can better use the intellect for what it was intended, instead of it using us.

"Let the Goddess Dance" public access television show in Los Angeles with some of the Seasons drumming workshop members performing: from the left, Ruth, Marilyn, Buddy, Cat, Brian, and Cathy.

19

TEAMWORK

Providing a drumming workshop or classes is a good investment for companies and corporations because it is an effective way of encouraging teamwork. It's that simple. When even total strangers get together and drum, they agree on many things.

One thing they agree on is quite abstract. It is the downbeat. When people begin to play together they don't give a thought to what an amazing act of selfless cooperation they are involved in. The downbeat, in a sense, is this great abstract blob of nothingness hanging outside of ourselves, right there in the middle of the drumming group. It is invisible and many times unheard, yet it exerts control and coherence over all of the participants, and, without fighting it, ideally we all accept its overall unquestionable authority.

The downbeat is what we listen for as we weave the grooves and bend the beats. The downbeat is what we all get back to after trying out our own experiments in rhythm. The downbeat is what we all try to maintain while others are flailing and wailing. This common definition of "Where's One?" is what holds us together. It does not matter if the players are from different cultures, different economic strata, or different religions. This common agreement to accept the downbeat as our basic point of departure melds everyone together into a functioning unit. And it doesn't even exist. It is merely an expedient, an agreed upon point of common ground that can be forgotten as soon as the drumming group is over.

But the amazing thing is that it is not forgotten entirely when the drumming is done. Total strangers smile at each other, sharing the few moments when they were unaware of each other's differences. This feeling they take with them. They remember this feeling. It is not a concept. It is not political or dogmatic. It is too simple for that. Yet it works the world over.

When I was asked to play drums in a palm grove in Bali, Indonesia, a carver came up from the back of the compound, sat down next to me, and picked up a drum. He could not speak my language and I could not speak Indonesian, yet we played together all afternoon. The group of people who had gathered around and participated were reluctant to stop and go back to work. We were so happy that it was difficult to finally stop. No words, just rhythm. I'll remember that afternoon for the rest of my life. I bet he will too.

This has happened time and time again in drumming groups when people of different cultural and economic and social backgrounds get together to play the drums. They suddenly start looking at each other with new eyes. They are actually seeing another human being who is a drummer, rather than an object to be pigeonholed. This happens even when people are struggling to play. They come from distant places in their souls to the drum in search of healing. It's as if this were the watering hole where mortal enemies congregate to share the mutual sustenance of the rhythmic currents. It's a safe zone.

When this experience is taken back into the real world there is an acceptance by the participants that it was special and unique. In that space, they were on some kind of equal footing with someone who otherwise would not have come into their lives. This creates a willingness among people to listen and accept what someone else, a total stranger or a friend, has to offer. If it is a rhythmic contribution to the group, then it is taken at face value. Does it work? Or doesn't it work? We can all hear immediately if it does. If someone's contribution does not work in a group, then this is a moment of truth, and that can be painful and even devastating.

photo: Cathleen Javier

Drum makers in a Bali village packed for shipment back to the U.S. the large and small dragon drums the author purchased. These are ceremonial, two-headed "Dolak"-style drums, used in the Ketchak Exorcism Dance. The heads are made of lizard skin, from the very large, Komodo Dragon-type lizards native to an island in the vicinity. While my drums were being packed, I played with a local carver/ drummer in front of this obscure little shop in the Balinese village. Everyone came out and we had a festival that afternoon.

One woman came to our workshop and tentatively played a conga drum, not interfering with the overall feel until she began to gain confidence. Then she decided to cut loose. At first she almost had it. Her improvisational licks got close, but tended to drift off the beat. This threw everyone else into confusion, forcing them to reestablish the downbeat before any of the others could try their own little improvisations. Each time this person took a break (a solo), everyone else tried to hold the beat together, but she played so loudly and unsteadily that everyone was struggling and having very little fun. Finally, I stopped the group and explained what was happening. She said that she had been with a boyfriend who was a drummer years earlier and she had listened to his Tito Puente records. Thus she had some ear for the drum licks, but she didn't have the etiquette to go with it. Tito Puente is one of the greatest drummers in the world, often emulated but never really duplicated, even by other great drummers. She listened to my gentle explanation, then said she was so embarrassed that she would never come again. Which she didn't. Too bad, but it was a relief for the rest of the group. They went on their merry way without her. She might some day realize that the fun that Tito can generate is as part of a whole band, not just as a soloist. She hadn't come to the understanding that she had to give support for the other players to do just what she was trying to do. Being a team player is what this is all about. The journey is personal, but the effort is by the group. This is what indigenous cultures have always known about drumming. They create a rhythmic environment that supports the personal enlightenment, but they always pay close attention to maintaining this group environment, many times replacing tired drummers with fresh drummers without losing the beat, continuing the ceremonies for days, even weeks. That's teamwork.

Q: What do you call the people who hang out with famous musicians?

A: Drummers.

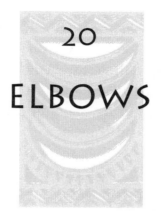

20

ELBOWS

I mentioned earlier the basic thirteen American rudiments and how they are to be played open and closed; that means slowly, then very fast, then slowly again. I learned this from my teacher when I was about nine years old, but I realized only recently that it was a form of active meditation.

Mrs. Trafford, my first drum teacher, was a woman with a great amount of presence in her personality as well as her drumming style. She could play anything. She had a whole house full of percussion instruments—three floors full of drums, marimbas, tympani, glockenspiel, tenor drums, snare drums, claves, bongos, congas. You name it in the world of drums, it was there.

Every week I showed up with my notebook with last week's lesson, and a real sense of dread if I had not practiced enough. The lesson would usually start out with a review of my rudiments. She would make notes like a therapist as I played my paradiddles or flam taps or ratamacues or whatever. Serious business, because come competition time, I would have to stand in front of three

An anthropologist was sitting next to the chief of a cannibal tribe deep in the jungle. They were eating and listening to the drummers. They sat there for a very long time listening to the drummers just going at it.

"Do the drummers ever stop?" asked the anthropologist.

The chief shook his head. "Bad things happen when drums stop," the chief said ominously.

They listened for a very long time. Finally the anthropologist interjected wearily.

"What could possibly be that bad? They've been playing for days!"

"When the drumming stops," the chief finally said, "then there's a bass solo."

state judges and perform whatever rudiments they asked of me, as well as a difficult drumming piece that I had been practicing. This was a great deal of pressure.

Eileen Trafford provided her students with a great tool to let go of the pressure. It was her method of breathing and relaxing while performing the rudiments. It took me out of my self-consciousness, into the realm of pure sound and sensation. The judges, the other competitive drummers, the world in general ceased to exist. Only the sound of the drum, the movement of the sticks in my hands, and the great overwhelming feel of physical rhythm carried me along.

When playing a rudiment like the paradiddle, which goes R–L–R–R, then L–R–L–L slowly, then gradually faster and faster, the individual notes cease to exist and a great roaring gush of pulsating sound engulfs the player and listener. The challenge for the player is to stay relaxed enough to attain the speed of light, which is where the rudiment finally sounds correct. At this incredible speed there is only the movement and the sound. When starting slowly, the first note is accented; PAR-a-did-dle, PAR-a-did-dle. But when the speeding-up process gets to the point where the individual notes are too close together to think about, my teacher explained to me to not think about the notes, to just think about my elbows. I watched her beefy elbows swing out, then in, then out again at the beginning accent of each paradiddle. It was almost a flapping motion, like dancing the Funky Chicken. She explained that when I get going so fast, my brain cannot keep up, so in order to make sure I'm doing it right, just concentrate on moving my elbows in and out, faster and faster, while I pay almost no attention to what my hands were doing. Just listen for that first accent note and don't worry about the smaller notes. It worked. Whereas normally, I would speed up, get tense, and hit the wall, unable to go any faster, I could now cease to think about the individual notes and just concentrate on moving my elbows in and out. This, coupled with her suggestion to breathe out, releasing the tension while I was playing, created a state of active relaxation. This state is familiar to anyone involved in sports or martial arts where speed is contingent on relaxation. This great dichotomy of speed and relaxation while exerting force is at the heart of this active meditation that has served me well in many different areas of life—not just drumming.

photo: Cathleen Javier

This large master talking drum from Ghana was carved from the trunk of a single tree by Alexander, a friend of Jumoke and Papa.

21

GOD IS IN YOUR SACRUM

Many yogis talk about the white light rushing into their brains when they are in certain meditation postures. One reason for this rush of enlightenment is the clearing up of blockages in the spinal sheath; both physical and emotional. This then enables the life force, the bioelectrical energy that runs our bodies, to travel unimpeded upwards from the sacrum to the brain. This rush of new energy is somewhat like getting our arteries cleared out, except that in the spinal envelope that fluid is salt water, not blood, and it carries electrical impulses up and down our spine. Certain muscle movements, such as yogi postures, unclog the blockages along the spinal envelope. These blockages are locked into different muscles surrounding our spine. When the muscle blocks are cleared through yoga, or chiropractics, or dance, the electrical flow is powerful. This is experienced in the brain as a white light, or some other kind of inspirational flash. I'm not discounting the possibility of actual Divine inspiration. I'm just talking about helping it along by freeing up the highway that it travels on in our bodies.

Drumming engenders movement, that movement is dance, and dance is what can free up the spinal sheath. Movement has been shown to have an effect on trauma locations in the spinal sheath. Moving to rhythm is an integrating process that not only releases some of the memory, but also replaces it with a more positive imprint. This isn't a substitute for therapy, but it is a lot more fun and it deals directly, on a physical level, with the locations of trauma.

The physical sensation of having to move when the beat is really good is a healthy response. It doesn't have to be suppressed. By moving to rhythm, muscle and synapse processes are stimulated, sometimes for the first time.

This can be a joyful discovery, but it can also be discomforting. That is why I always encourage people to take it easy on themselves when they are trying to play a drum. Tension sets in if the inner critic is working. The tension prevents the drumming rhythm from flowing smoothly. The whole process then becomes an intellectual exercise. However, when the player can just feel the rhythm, playing along without judging, then the natural healing properties of the rhythm can do their work.

The source of this inspirational power is known to be in the sacrum. This is also the location of the first and lowest chakra. That is the lower cluster of small bones at the base of our spines. This grouping of bones can ideally act as a pump, forcing the fluid up through the envelope all the way to the brain. In most of us, this pump is calcified and rigid so it cannot pump the life-carrying fluid up to the brain. The trauma that we have all experienced in our lives are imprinted on the spinal sheath. These imprints of negative electrical locations twist the sheath and restrict the flow of fluid. Movement can loosen up the sacrum, along with chiropractics and other forms of treatment, but, to some degree, the mere act of dancing can create a better flow of divine energy from the sacrum up to the brain. When this flow is open, we experience the white light that the yogis talk about. This is not a substitute for yoga, but is just another way to help us along into a better, more integrated attitude toward life.

When I first received what was then called "Network" chiropractics, I was shown a patient lying peacefully on an adjustment table in a darkened room. After the doctor had given the woman a light touching treatment, she let the woman lay still to process the treatment. In a moment, the woman let out a big sigh and her spine started to undulate in a most graceful wave. It traveled down from her head to her pelvis, then back up again. There was no tension or drastic movements. It was the spine adjusting itself. At that moment I realized the healing power of rhythmic movement all over again. I could do that with drumming. I had always been able to get people to move and dance. That's when I knew that I had to record a drumming CD, so I recorded "Drum Dance" as a way to engender gentle movement in a person so that their own spine could heal itself as mine did. My need to find a way to contribute to the world in a positive way was answered out of an injury that was a blessing in disguise.

A drummer is a musician's best friend.

photo: Lynne Alexander

Buddy holds the downbeat with a tambourine on his foot at drumming workshops along the Gulf Coast, including St. Petersburg and Sarasota, Florida, August 1998. This group grew from just a few people to over a hundred.

22

IMPROVISATION
AND INSPIRATION

There is a goal to all of this thought and study. That goal might be to stop thinking and working so hard and just be creative. Creativity is a flowing of ideas that ideally occurs in the artist without self-consciousness. The criticism can come later if need be, but during the actual creative process a miraculous state of being occurs; it is a selfless, nondefined freedom in our souls. This breath of fresh air blows through our busy conscious mind and clears away the detritus of the day. In some cases it heals old wounds and in special circumstances unites us with a gestalt of human history of the world and the Universe.

There are myriad ways of achieving this state of clarity and soul connection. Meditations, yoga, therapies, the arts, religion, the list can go on. Sometimes this state hits like a lightning bolt from heaven. Other times the selfless state of pure creativity occurs only after a painstaking trek up a mountain of training and study. The different levels of this profound change in our thinking are as different as people are, although there are schools of thought that have codified certain levels of Samadhi or awareness. Every culture has had devotees who could find their own ways of achieving this oneness that is paradoxically also selflessness. By oneness, I mean that it is a personal sensation. It is something that the individual experiences. What has this got to do with drumming?

If done in the right spirit, drumming is a vehicle and a tool to find this state of clarity and peace. It can also be used to achieve other effects, but this process that brings us closer to the divine is what we're about in our workshops.

Some people may ask, "I don't know if I'm 'there.' I doubt my own intuition so much that I can't even tell if I've achieved enlightenment. Am I doing it right?"

Generally my advice is along the lines of, "Don't work so hard. Don't think about it. Just have fun." This is not to stress just the fun aspects. It is to give the player something else to distract themselves with, instead of looking at their own predicament too closely. After all we are going for a state of being where the self is not the most important thing. One reason that drumming can work so well as a tool for creativity is that there are signals that tell us if we are doing it right.

First of all, if we start to smile, then we are on the right track. Inherent joy is an element in the process of divine enlightenment. Another clue is that we realize that we are not working hard; that what we are playing is effortless. This occurs when the body and mind have achieved a détente of intention—when there is no struggle between intellect and action. More tellingly, we know when we're right, when the damned thing starts to swing. This has been what motivates musicians since the beginning of time. It's why so many musicians play for free or for almost no money, or get ripped off for their music; they're getting so much from just swinging that the money is of absolutely no consequence. In fact, some musicians feel guilty for getting the money because they're having so much fun just playing. The purist sees the money as a distraction, but the audience needs to see that magic in the players. They pay to experience that creative state, at least vicariously. The audience gets a mere hint of the joy that the player experiences, but that hint is so profound that we create stars out of players who are just doing what they love to do.

This state of creative flow is available to all of us. We do not have to be standing on a stage, under the lights and playing through a loud sound system. We need to be with our own spirits and feel the grooves of the universe. The ego has absolutely nothing to do with this state of grace. It usually gets in the way. I've heard so many successful players say that they wish they could get back to that state of being they lost along the road to success—when they were able to just play, their original way of being before the platinum records. It may be lost, but it can be regained.

But all of the talk about higher states of consciousness is still a smoke screen for the ultimate effect of drumming. That special effect that I see as worth more than gold and fame is the ability to improvise with the universe, to play with confidence and grace in each moment of the rhythm. To become a fearless improvisor. To step into the unknown with confidence and joy, trusting that the universe is right there with you—on your groove, swinging like there's no tomorrow, and each note that you play fits so right that there is no question about good or better. This does not come from "heavy chops," or fast licks, or good-looking hair moves. It can be just the downbeat and nothing more. It can be the subtlest shaker part being played as accompaniment to someone else's soloing. It can come from just clapping your hands.

Back in the seventies, I was touring with Tim Buckley, and we had a night off in San Francisco. I took my girlfriend to see Rahsaan Roland Kirk at a small jazz club called Keystone Korner. The place was packed. We had no reservations. The huge Black bouncer at the door surveyed this skinny White kid with muttonchops and his blonde date and urged us to go find a different venue. I insisted. He finally said there were only two seats, down by the edge of the stage, right next to the dressing room door, at the bottom of the steps leading up to the stage. "Are you kidding? Of course we'll take them," I said eagerly.

Rahsaan had a great band; Jack Dejohnette was on drums. I don't remember the rest of the band, although there was a nerdy White guy playing one of the first mini Moog synthesizers. He huddled over the keyboard while Roland Kirk made fun of him and urged him to "play them blues, boy!" Roland Kirk seemed angry. I think he usually seemed angry. It was part of his music. He was blind and a genius. That's enough to make anyone angry. He wore his trademark, thick wraparound shades and a dark suit. He seemed to glisten under the purple lights. He was dripping with horns. His soprano hung on one strap, his Stritch on another, his Saxello was duct-taped together so that he could play two horns at once. He leaned into the mike and growled, "We ain't playin' no jazz. You want to get jazzed, go on down to the red-light district. We playin' black classical music." And with that threat he took off on a *tour de force* of the history of Black classical music in America; New Orleans, St. Louis, Chicago, New York, and all points in between. He played his flute like a machine gun. I looked around us and wondered why he always shot the audience

"We ain't playin' no jazz. You want to get jazzed, go on down to the red-light district. We playin' black classical music."

—*Rahsaan*

with his flute. Then I thought that maybe he was just shooting the white folks. This night, that meant just Cathleen and me. Not that it mattered; what he was doing was inspirational beyond color and gender. As the finale, the bass player laid down his upright and picked up a baritone sax and pumped out a gospel bass line while he stepped down off the stage in front of us. Rahsaan followed the sound, playing his tenor sax like a demon. It was an up-tempo Gospel groove and he was putting every kind of music on top of it. Dejohnette was cooking on the drums on stage. Rahsaan listened and followed the baritone out through the audience, and eventually out of the club's front door, all the while playing like he was possessed. I grabbed Cathleen's hand and pulled her with me. This was too important to miss. We moved through the crowd, which remained seated. They were staying cool and grooving, but I was on fire. The bouncer stopped us at the door and wouldn't let us go out, but he let us stand there and watch Rahsaan standing in the middle of the intersection, playing up into the night. The sound of his tenor sax multiplied in volume and harmonics as the notes blasted up the concrete walls of the surrounding apartment buildings. People leaned out of their windows and yelled down at him. "Shut up! I'm trying to sleep!"

A San Francisco police car sat quietly at the curb and just watched. The image of Roland Kirk straddling the street and wailing up into the San Francisco night was burned into my brain. His sound echoed down my spine like it was a fire alarm. Then the two men turned around, still playing that Gospel up-tempo jump, and came back into the club. Cathleen and I went back to our seats, clapping along with a lot of the others in the crowd. As Roland came by us, he stopped and turned to me. He was playing furiously, sweat dripping off of him. He heard my hand claps and decided to just stand there and play his horn in my face. His bell was inches from my nose. It lasted for a long time, I lost track. I was just clapping my hands. He was playing like a mad man. Nothing else existed. Finally he stepped back up onto the stage, and ended the set. He left the stage and that was the end of it. A young black woman friend of his was sitting next to us and before she went back to the dressing room, she asked if we would come back tomorrow night. She had a look of newfound interest. I shrugged, I was back out on the road the next night, working myself. She looked into my eyes and said simply, "Take care." That was all it took to share that bright moment. That inspirational moment is obviously still with me and it came from just hand claps.

In Arabic countries, a master transfers their inspirational energy directly to their students. It's called "Baraka" or blessings. This person to person transference is required in some doctrines as the only acceptable way for a student of a master to be acknowledged as the heir to the master's teachings. I don't play saxophone, but I got a whole lot of something that night.

The next day, back on tour, I told Tim Buckley about my epiphany at the night club and he laughed, always the seasoned road warrior. "I played with Roland Kirk a few years ago," Timmy said. "We were all on stage with Frank Zappa and the Mothers of Invention at the Filmore. Everyone was soloing, but Frank came over to Roland Kirk and tried to tell him what to play. Roland said, 'This ain't the plantation no more, man,' and he went on playing what he wanted to play."

photo: Teri Smith

Buddy playing "Sally Go Round the Roses" with Tim Buckley at the Starwood, Hollywood, California, in 1975.

23

VOLUME

Try playing softer. It will sound much better. No need to get carried away and play as hard as you can. It doesn't make you a better drummer and it annoys the neighbors. Volume goes up when people are not paying attention. They start to play louder to be heard over someone else who isn't listening. It's a vicious circle.

If some people remember to play softer, sometimes the others will tone down, but that's rare, so just yell, "Play softer!"

The misconception is that a groove only works when it is being played with all the muscle you can muster. Grooves work when there is room left on top to go somewhere with the volume. "Dynamics" are what musicians call it. This subtle part of music was lost with the advent of amplifiers.

One new drummer in our workshop came from Brooklyn and he was amazed that we could play just as intensely at a soft volume. He said, "I realized that I was being selfish." He hit the nail on the head much sooner than some of the sea-soned veterans.

Of course, men tend to play louder than women; they tend to do everything louder than women. This is no excuse. Men are usually the instigators of playing louder. Before you know it, the volume is too loud to hear. That's all well and good, but the kind of drumming that a lot of people *want* to do is softer, more subtle, closer to the groove, and generally more pleasant. These are usually the more meditative personalities, so they are generally overwhelmed by the louder, less sensitive players who couldn't care less if the wimps played or not. All I can suggest is that the softer players must band together and take back control of their drumming group from the bashers rather than continue to be victims. Life is like drumming. There have been some really loud women players in the workshops too; they're cutting loose after years of repression. This can lead a person into a different kind of drumming; where the drum becomes a symbol of whoever oppressed them. That's okay too, only in a group of drummers, everyone has to hit the same kind of thing. That's what the magic in drumming is all about—that focus of intent. Being a victim of one's own past while playing a drum is really not the point. I can see when someone goes inside of themselves and just bashes the drum. They stop looking around the group, they internalize every-thing. Sometimes it's a selfish act. Sometimes it's necessary, but that kind of mindset makes it difficult to communicate with the other drummers who are not beating the drum as a symbol of a painful past, but just as a drum in a group. There can be a lot of reasons why people hit the drum too hard. Just remember that force isn't the answer.

It's easier for everyone to hear when the volume is at a manageable level. Subtle parts have an important effect and can get lost in the bombast.

In indigenous cultures, volume isn't as much an issue. They don't have a need to play louder, and there is no anxiety about the silence. Of course they aren't playing chamber music either. The legendary talking drums across Africa actually do carry messages from one village to another, and from one tribal area to the next. It is a poetry of rhythm, using higher and lower notes. Traditionally, African languages did not have words for higher pitched notes and lower pitched notes, they defined notes as penetrating and passive or masculine and feminine.

Early anthropologists tried to document the primitive rhythms that mysteriously conveyed information across miles of open wilderness. Through translators they asked odd questions like, "What is your musical scale like? How do you know if a spoken word will correspond to a high note or a low note?" The concept of high note and low note did not translate; high is the sky, low is the earth. Why confuse matters? Many times a higher note would be penetrating and that note could be defined as a masculine note. The lower, more passive note would be a feminine note, but then in a different moment, the opposite would be true. This is an entirely different type of definition from the way we think about higher and lower notes.

We are looking for the grooves—the rhythmic patterns that will connect us to our own sources of inspiration.

The main village drum was a wooden slit drum cut from a section of a large, hollowed-out tree. The tone played by a masterful interpreter could send a message of penetrating and passive notes maybe fifteen miles or more.

We do not have to send a drum message across the jungle today stating, "White hunters on the way," but we still are the

White hunters. Only now, instead of hunting for the white rhino, the cheetah, or the elephant, we are looking for the grooves—the rhythmic patterns that will connect us to our own sources of inspiration. And this may bring a little peace in the valley.

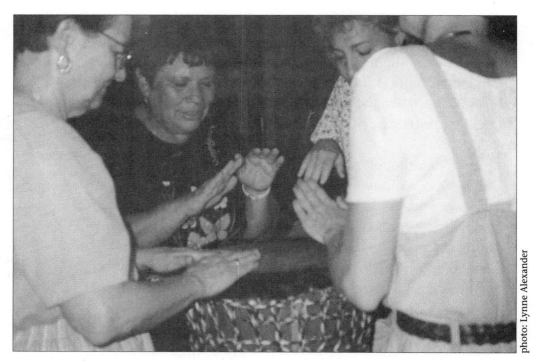

photo: Lynne Alexander

These four women have found the groove, and happily share one drum.

24

HEARING

Most of the time, a beginning player's inability to perform a certain pattern is not because they cannot technically perform the sequence of notes; it is because their ears are not paying attention.

Most of our ears assume they are doing a good job. "Don't bother me, I'm hearing good enough." It is a humbling reality check for the ears to realize that they are not hearing precisely the right spaces and notes in a given pattern. So don't become discouraged when what you play does not sound right. If you are trying to hit a certain syncopated note at just the right spot but are not getting it, it has more to do with hearing than hand dexterity.

Okay, here is a lesson for the folks who want to learn something. Let's pretend we're playing a four-beat pattern. That means we count to four, then repeat ourselves, counting up to four each time the pattern repeats itself. You know—one, two, three, four, one, two, three, four, etc. Now let's pretend that we're really busy drummers and we'll play all the notes that are possible; that's not just the one, two, three, four, beats, but all the beats in between those big beats. For the sake of simplicity, we'll play four notes for each beat. That's a lot of notes. It's very busy sounding. There's no space for variations. It sounds like a machine. We play four notes for each four beats. Math is part of drumming if you want to be that kind of drummer. Four beats times four notes per beat equals sixteen. That's what musicians call those fast little notes: sixteenth notes. My first drum teacher, Eileen Trafford taught me to count it like this: "One de and da Two de and da Three de and da Four de and da," then repeat again. If we were to play all these possible notes we would hear a steady stream of evenly placed pats on the drumhead. Our ears would hear an even and steady pattern. Pretty soon, this repeating pattern would get boring and our ears would cease to distinguish all the notes individually. Our hearing would check into this repetitious activity whenever it thought it needed to in order to keep it going. Again, it is a survival habit of the brain that needs to be dealt with.

Now, while playing this repeating, even pattern of notes on the drumhead, hit the first note on the ONE beat harder. It becomes an accent. Now suddenly the picture changes. The ear now bases every other beat on that accent. Every time that ONE beat comes around, you accent it. So far so good? That is the downbeat and our ear is handling that alright.

In our technological culture, everything is sort of based on the downbeat. This is a holdover in part from a militaristic society where everybody marches to the downbeat. We have been convinced that the world functions on the downbeat—at least this world. In reality, there are all kinds of syncopation or upbeats. That means that there are accents on beats that are not the downbeat. How's the boring drum pattern going? Are you still playing it nice and steady and accenting the *one* beat?

Now here's where it gets interesting and where your ears are left standing at the ten-second line, because it gets faked out by the great syncopated moves of a Michael Jordan.

While continuing to play the steady pattern, now add a second accent on the "da" beat. Say and play: "One de and DA Two de and da Three de and da Four de and da, One de and DA Two de and da Three de and da Four de and da, One de and DA Two de and da Three de and da Four de and da, etc."

A number of things are going through your brain at this point—first of all, panic. Don't panic, it's just a drumbeat.

Your attention is interrupted when you hit that funny accent and you probably stop playing right after you hit that accent on the "da" of the one. That happens when your brain thinks it's finished its task. It just stops and says, "There. I'm done." But what must happen is that you should continue to play the steady pattern right past that special accent note that your brain was so proud of playing. So, the first lesson to learn here is to keep playing the steady pattern while hitting that funny accent. Don't stop. What is happening from your ear's point of view is this: "Okay, I hit the accent and now my job is over, I'll take a vacation until the next accent." It forgets that there is the other task of playing the continuous pattern. So, don't stop when you hit the accent, keep playing the next note, which is on the Two beat.

This splits your attention up into two different activities; One activity is to play the steady repeating pattern and the second activity is to hit the accents. This may be a new experience for some of us because we have been tricked into believing that our attention is an all or nothing proposition, meaning that we usually focus our attention wholly and completely on the task at hand and when that task is finished our attention goes to the next task. In the case of drumming our attention does two tasks at the same time. In drumming this is sometimes called "independence." This refers to the independent actions of our different limbs. It's why Buddy Rich could play two bass drums and have both hands going at the same time, playing entirely different things, and grinning and yelling at his band members at the same time. He started at an early age to break up his attention span and do various tasks at the same time. He was drumming professionally at the age of eighteen months, so don't be hard on yourself if this process doesn't come to you right away. Its the amazing way in which our brains work that is fascinating to me.

Q: How do you get a drummer to stop playing?

A: Make them read the music.

I want to remind you that this pattern is not technically hard to play. It is just hard to hear because of our assumptions about reality. Our ears have insisted that all accents fall on the downbeat. Here, the accent is falling on the most insignificant beat; the last da after the downbeat: "One de an DA." How frustrating for our omnipotent ears to be forced into hearing something that is too "insignificant to really be of any importance at all."

But when it happens, when you begin to hear better, hear more precisely, then your hands will follow and you will begin to feel the accent. When this happens, the ear has gotten the message and it is now willing to play and learn. This is when the fun begins. It has nothing to do with hot licks and fast notes and lightning-fast wrists. The feel has more to do with paying attention.

This ability to hear syncopated patterns is an endangered ability in the human organism, but it's always been endangered. Back when anthropologists were first visiting Africa and listening to the tribal drumming, they could not hear the sophistication of rhythms. Their hearing had been so limited to the downbeat as the only accent that their brains were unable to distinguish the subtle play of syncopations that is the poetry of African rhythms. These visitors from a differently structured society had blinders on their ears. They decided that what they were hearing was utter chaos. Too bad.

This type of blindness is typical in our culture today. There is a homogenization of the world's varied beats into something that is manageable and danceable and saleable, even to the most rigid of people.

This is called pop music. It's the quest for the perfect hook line, the perfect beat, the most common of lyrics, and the most nondescript melody, all for the sake of being "commercial." The human ear has become so spoiled that any kind of rough edge on the music is almost frightening and strange. The eagerness to hear new sounds and rhythms is an acquired taste these days. If we don't wake up our ears, we would all just settle for the same old thing. If that were the case, we'd still be dancing like our great-great grandparents.

Here is another exercise to try. First, just hit the drum evenly, using both hands going back and forth. Now, instead of counting four beats and hitting an accent, try counting three beats and hit an accent. Weird, right? It happens on your "sleeping hand." I call your sleeping hand the good friend that you never knew you had. It's the hand that we do less with. For right-handed people, it would be their left hand, usually. For left-handed people it's different sometimes.

When we hit the drum, back and forth, using alternating hands, this sets up a certain signal to the brain, but when we accent every third note, it forces us to use our sleeping hand as an accent note. This is all very technical but when we play, it is nonverbal and fun.

This three-note pattern is called a "tripolet" in American drum culture. That's because we were concerned with only how the tripolet "fits" into a space normally reserved for more notes. It stretches three notes over a space normally filled by four notes. That was the mathematical examination of a much deeper phenomenon. Now we are discovering that it is the key to many meditational rhythms. Thinking in "three" is different.

Back to hitting the drum evenly, back and forth, hitting the drumhead with each hand equally. Accent every third note. It will hit first on your right hand, then it will hit on your left hand, then on your right hand, and then your left hand.

This sends equally strong signals to both sides of your brain from each hand. The brain makes assumptions about reality, which usually means that a right-handed person will think with their right hand most of the time. Drumming stimulates both sides of the brain in a very pleasant way, plus you discover that the really cool licks are based on your sleeping hand hitting the accents. Good luck—right? Really, it is possible. If I can do it, anybody can.

The amazing thing about the tripolet is that such a simple and basic rhythm can throw your brain into a stop mode when you are trying to understand it, or it can send you into a deep trance of profound feeling. The three-beat patterns can be combined with rhythms that don't seem right but still feel right—very loose and swinging rhythms that make you want to sway like water. It's a waltz in European music, but underneath that stiff three beat is the lurking passion of the Latin three beats that are found in the Quaquanco music of Cuba and the Bataka rhythms of Africa.

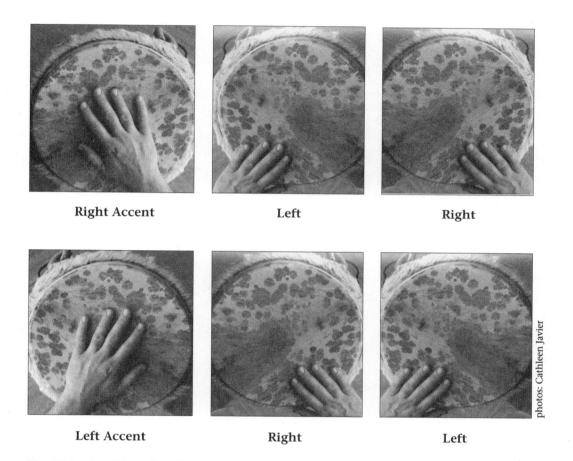

Right Accent   Left   Right

Left Accent   Right   Left

photos: Cathleen Javier

The Tripolet (three-beat) pattern alternates the accent beat from right to left hands. (See pp. 158–160 for more on this pattern.)

25

HABITS

Even the best players have habits. They fall back into tried and true rhythm patterns. They go on automatic pilot. A musician might be accused of "phoning in his part" during a performance because he was somewhere else instead of focused on the band. That's why it is so important to play with other people; you can learn other patterns and other ways to live and look at the world. They can bring you back from going on automatic pilot.

I suggest different ways to play a simple rhythm to some of the players in the workshop just to wake up different neuron pathways between the brain and the muscles, and also to wake up their lives. It's a refreshing stimulation to the body and mind that also changes the body's habitual way of reacting.

A dancer had been drumming with us. She had trouble waking up her "sleeping hand." The sleeping hand is a term from martial arts. Dan, Bruce Lee's old partner and master martial arts teacher, used the term, "dead hand" during one of our private drum lessons. I liked the concept of sleeping hand better than dead hand. It wasn't such a negative connotation. There was potential for change in the definition. In teaching, I don't use negative definitions unless really necessary. The "waking hand" is what I work for. We all have a sleeping hand as well as corresponding parts of our arm, body, brain, and our lives that are also asleep. The drum can wake us up.

Cat, the dancer who couldn't get her left hand to respond quickly enough, needed a structured way of reprogramming her muscles. She had the innate ability to play. It was more of an electrical adjustment to her nerves. So I gave her some tripolet patterns to play. Tripolets are three notes played as you say: "Trip-O-let-Trip-O-let, etc." The pattern is just back and forth from one hand to the other hand; right-left-right, left-right-left-etc. The interesting thing about tripolets is that every time you start the next tripolet, you start it on your other hand, your sleeping hand. Right-left-right is one tripolet. Then left-right-left is the next tripolet starting with your strong hand, then right-left-right, then left-right-left. It doesn't matter if you are right handed or left handed, every time you do the second tripolet, you exercise your sleeping hand. Your brain may seize up when you try this because it gets in the way. If you don't think about it, you can go right-left-right-left until the cows come home without any anxiety level at all. But, when you think about each three-note tripolet, suddenly you must wake up your sleeping hand, your sleeping brain, your sleeping life. Easy to play, but hard to think about. Yet, it's just three notes, or better yet, six notes tied together; that way you think about your sleeping hand starting every other tripolet. A steady constant tripolet pattern is what you want to get to.

When I was a boy, I met Buddy Rich and asked him, "How much do you practice?"

He laughed and said. "I don't practice. I play."

Most people try to get through life using only one hand, half of their body and their minds. Maybe half of their souls. We usually forget that we're using less than half of what we could be playing with unless someone comes along and tells us to "Take it!" Then we might wake up.

"Take it!" might be yelled at a musician on stage at anytime by the singer or the band leader. This can happen at an unexpected moment. Like when the singer realizes that his fly is open. He turns around and yells at the drummer to "Take it!" so the singer can adjust his wardrobe. The person being singled out must take a solo—immediately. Not only must they take a solo right away, but they must make it sound good, and look good too. That's show bizness. It's also a major anxiety situation. What if you were walking down the street and a stranger yells at you: "Take it!"

Are you ready to solo at a moment's notice? Few people are. But that's what life is to a player; you "comp" behind the singer and the soloist (that means you are supporting the singer or soloist with unobtrusive chord rhythm), then perhaps you take a solo yourself, the band then ends the tune together, the crowd loves it, and the musicians get paid for the gig. But there is always that possibility that you'll be required to solo at an unexpected time when you're not really feeling like soloing. The show must go on. Life must go on. Improvising can be an analogy for solving life's problems, immediately.

The three-beat pattern isn't something we're used to in this technological culture. We are more familiar with four-beat patterns. I think our modern society has been running on four beat patterns. The four-stroke internal combustion engine is a good example of a cultural metronome. The three-beat pattern is used in many cultures for meditation exercises. It can be simple and also compelling.

I gave the dancer a tripolet pattern to play. I stressed that she shouldn't "practice it," just play it. Practice is no fun. Playing is. I encourage people to play instead of practicing. When I was a boy, I met Buddy Rich and asked him, "How much do you practice?" He laughed and said, "I don't practice. I play."

Cat worked on the three-beat tripolet pattern and it seemed to help. She began to use her left hand in a variety of ways. Then she began to use her left foot much more. This surprised her. She began dance steps with her left foot, opening up a whole new world of movement for her. I'm sure brain functions also changed. This was part of a major change in her life too. She seemed to be more balanced; left and right sides were functioning more evenly.

This analogy transfers into regular life. By stepping out with our sleeping foot, or doing something with our sleeping hand, we become integrated in a small but important way. The functions between the right and left halves of our brain exchange energies in a new way. Learning keeps us young and flexible.

This carries over into our life, where it seems we always need to improvise in this ever-changing world. When we can use a new, creative problem-solving method in our brains we can stay ahead of the game or at least stay in the game. Moving with the flow of the already existing beat of life is possible when we don't panic or resist, and creating new and unusual ways to interpret that flow keeps us alive, learning, improvising, and dancing.

Playing at the Surfer's Club in 1965. I first discovered the power of
The Beat as the kids danced to the music of "Those Five," my high
school band. It was an incredible rush of awareness and power to
actually see all the kids bouncing up and down in unison to our
beat in the Madiera Beach Teen Club. I could look out a picture
window at the empty night beach and glowing, phosphorous waves
of the Gulf of Mexico. It was a mystical experience that you could
dance to.

26

LET THE GODDESS DANCE

A woman approached me after a very deep drumming workshop in a church. She had been listening to the group and had at some point felt safe enough to get up and dance. She moved with an interpretive grace and filled the holes in the rhythms with her own body movements. She became a vessel for the rhythm to express itself for all of us to see. The dance helped the drummers find the right feel. When she approached me after we had finished she simply thanked me for creating a safe space for her to dance. That's when I realized another very important reason for the drum. That's also where the title for this book came into my head.

Now that we know how to play and carry a groove, what happens next? Dance is what happens next.

This magical thing that we have discovered, this ability to get ourselves to feel and respond, is really a tool for something else. The drum is a tool for the dance. If we play it right—with just the right amount of energy, not too fast, not too slow, not too many notes, the right holes,, and not too loud and not too proud—then we feel like dancing to the beat.

When the feel is so effortless that it is not work, but merely play, then it is time to dance. When the members of the group are listening to each other while playing, when the group supports each member in their efforts to grow and explore the world of rhythm, then it will feel like dance music. When the basic pattern is held steady and the beat does not speed up, then it will feel good enough to dance to. When the ego of the players allows the truth to come pouring out, then there will be dance.

When this flowing of creative energy is filling up the space and giving us the feeling that there is a safe and special place, then the dance will come. When this dance energy does arrive, we must learn to respect it.

When we know how to play and carry a groove, dance happens.

I spent many years of my life creating a dance beat for people—in nightclubs, in bars, in public places, gymnasiums, roller rinks, football stadiums, arenas, coliseums, festivals, cow pastures, swamps, forests, recording studios, television shows, and sound stages. It was a great sense of power to see everyone moving to the beat that I was playing. It took me many years to accept this power and to understand it somewhat. The greatest mystery is what happens to the dancer when the dance beat begins. The person dancing becomes lost to this time and this place. They are communing with a deep source of creativity that needs to be protected.

Too many times I have seen a woman, in the throes of ecstatic communion with the rhythmic flow, suddenly be harassed by a man who thinks she is asking for sex. This need by men to intervene, to interrupt, and to steal this energy is at the foundation of the problem that we are dealing with today in our modern culture.

Primitive cultures can let a woman dance to invoke the creative spirit. We must learn to do the same. Otherwise this creative energy will turn foul and bitter. It will grow destructive. In the Hindu worldview, the female energy is divided into the creative and the destructive. When the feminine energy is creative, we all benefit. When the creative is frustrated, it turns destructive and we all suffer. The great challenge for men today is to recognize the necessity for women and men to be left alone in their rapture of the rhythm. When a woman is dancing, she is not necessarily asking for sex. She is involved in a spiritual activity that should not be interrupted. Men witnessing this event can be blessed with the energy that is flowing through the dancers, as long as they don't interrupt it. In certain rituals with drum and dance, the person being "ridden" by the deity must be treated with great respect. They will go through the movements characteristic of the deity that has inhabited them for the length of the ceremony. In exchange the other people receive blessings from this deity.

Drumming and trance go hand in hand. We need trance in our personal lives as a way of escaping to the other realms for recuperation, healing, wisdom, inspiration, and rebirth, as well as to receive truly sacred knowledge that is unspeakable and unnameable. The drum brings us to the doors of these perceptions. Our own attitude carries us through and decides what we are able to bring back.

The journey is the adventure. The song is in the playing. The beat is in the dancing. The joy is in the laughing. The drum is in your hands. Let the Goddess dance.

photo: Cathleen Javier

The Ocean is rhythm. It's something you can't control, yet you can ride it—Buddy on Staircase Beach at Malibu, sunset, New Year's Day, 2000.

27

ATTENTION DEFICIT DISORDER

The condition that has been labeled "attention deficit disorder" includes a lot of symptoms that are present for many people. Drumming in the right spirit brings this splintered attention gently into focus with a pleasurable reward for the sincere ADD person. Our attention will wander even under the best of conditions, but while playing the drum, it is obvious when that happens. The player then reconnects to the downbeat and the feel. This is accomplished without any remorse or guilt. That is very important for the student, because a sense of anxiety gets in the way of learning for anyone. This way of reconnecting is both enjoyable and beneficial to the drummer's psyche, as well as to the group's sound.

The drum gives us a method to learn our own ways to stay focused on the downbeat. With the drum it is a physical process. The body has ways to compensate when the brain is being stubborn. The feel of the rhythms has a soothing effect on the ADD rush of awareness and distractions. With a short period of confidence building, the ADD person gets a great sense of accomplishment and group support. This is a way to see how the brain interferes with the body's innate ability to heal and play.

One day an art director in the movie business rushed into our store to pick up a beaded curtain he had ordered weeks earlier. He was agitated, tense, and having a hard time managing all the things that just *had* to get done. In the process, nothing got done. He seemed to have no peace of mind from which to make decisions. He exhibited the classic symptoms of ADD; he was distracted and very hard on himself. When I mentioned drumming, something seemed to connect for him. He sat down and played for just a few moments. He had never hit a drum before, but it took just a couple of beats and he was grounded and centered. He felt a sense of relief and calmness again. This is typical of how we are constantly distracted from our own peace of mind. The steady drum beat reconnects us to a sense of calmness.

28

DRUMMING
IN THE DARK

I was trapped on the L.A. freeway years ago, late for a recording session. When I arrived at the studio, I immediately sat down behind my Gretch drumset and we went straight into the song that was to be recorded. I was angry from the frustrations on the freeway and the spiritual limitations of the music biz, and it showed on the first take. The producer loved it, but it also scared him.

"You play really great when you're angry!" he enthused, a little tentatively.

He knew what a lot of drummers know about themselves. They play from an angry place. This is the kind of drumming that is used for war, for destruction, for forcing the world to listen to you. It can be a childish place, but it has the illusion of power. Many drummers like to go there because it is satisfying to feel that power. It is a false power, though, because it has only superficial effect. The effect seems real because it is the power that energizes people to go to war or to fight. It is the

169

kind of power in some punk rock or heavy metal, as well as in certain military music.

There is nothing wrong with this kind of drumming if it is done in its proper place. I loved the Sex Pistols. They were a hilariously angry band. Many people mistook the anger for real and took it to heart. The kids mistook the artistic expression of anger as the real thing, so they acted out their own scenarios of anger, and the result was vandalism and destruction and personal tragedy. I have seen the change in pop music, from "All You Need is Love" to "Pretty Vacant," from love to anger. This is a condition of our culture.

Anger is being sold to us as a commodity. It seems to be in everything we see and hear. It has become a habitual state of affairs. Maybe that is why I stress the peaceful side of drumming. There is a type of sacred drumming that creates a powerful destructive chord in the Universe: the Dance of Shiva in Hindu; the dance of destruction. The drum patterns for that state of chaos are special and secret. To play them, drummers must be well versed in personal control of their own emotions, because the drum beats can drive people wild. The problem is that it is addictive for some drummers. They get a taste of that power and they want to go there again and again. Many times drummers go there accidentally.

Drumming through the anger can be a healthy thing to do—moving through a feeling of anger into a wider acceptance of our place in the Universe. I have helped nurture some drumming groups over the years and have seen some of them taken over by angry drummers. I was there to some extent too, years ago, so I'm not condemning them. I want them to pass through this very primitive stage of drumming into a fuller understanding and respect of the power they have at their disposal. In order for this to happen the angry drummer needs to forgive. We need to forgive all the people we are angry at. We need to forgive ourselves and find a moment of peace in our souls. When this happens the real power comes through us.

This flow of power through the drummer is intoxicating and, to the novice, this power is misunderstood as their own power. It isn't seen as an outside blessing, but rather it is mistaken as their own way to get back at an uncaring Universe.

It is easy for some drummers to groove away and feel the meditative pulse of the Mother Earth, but it is not so easy for others who are being saturated with images of hate and anger all the time. This angrier mindset can change with time, but do we have the time?

I was angry, so angry that I couldn't even play drums. Now, I have come to realize that the drum also saved me from myself, from my own anger. That is the blessing I want to try to give to people.

The Chinese stress that a gong is to be hit after the drums are played so as to change the power of war into the power of peace.

A woman came into the shop and wanted to drum, but she was so shy and repressed that she couldn't even hit a drum. She was wealthy, so she bought a beautiful djembe from Ghana, Africa and took it home. There it sat and she didn't play it. Possessing it was her only way of drumming. She did try to come to a workshop, but she was so frightened that she stopped outside of the shop and didn't come in. I had no idea she was outside, holding her drum and unable to come in and play with the rest of us. Later, she came in by herself and we drummed. She said she felt better that way. When she finally did come into a group, she frowned and hit the drum like it was someone in her life that she wanted to beat up. The problem was that she couldn't hit the drum hard enough to get a tone. Her anger made her impotent and weak. When she laughed, she finally was able to get a good sound out of the drum. This didn't replace her anger, but it gave her a way to work with it.

We all have anger, to some degree, but the ability to articulate it is a way to diffuse its destructive power over us. The drum is a way to regain our own power over ourselves and over our own anger, by expressing it in a safe way through the drum.

Drumming through the anger gives us someplace to go with all that fire and drive. It gives us a place to end up. The goal is to work through the anger, find the peaceful solution, and resolve the pain into a healing song. If we don't end with a healing song, and instead end on a note of anger, then the world is left in that state of unresolved anger. The Chinese always stress that a gong is to be hit after the drums are played so as to change the power of war into the power of peace. We need to resolve our own violent natures into a tool for peace and healing. For centuries the drum has been used as a tool of war, an implement of the military machine.

I make a point not to play from an angry place when I am showing people how to use the drum. If we learn from a tense, angry place, then we play from that same tense, angry place.

The drum, in my eyes, is one of the most powerful tools in the world. Nations have gone to war driven by the beat of drums. Wars have also been ended with the beat of a peaceful drum.

Civilizations have been destroyed while the drum is beaten. Slaves were forced to work beyond their endurance to the beat of a drum. But the greatest and quietest creative healing has also worked through the drum.

I see the drum in a different light and I want to explain it so that other people can see that it is a powerful tool for healing and not just a loud tool for aggressive behavior.

The power of the drum is open to all people; it is an equal opportunity tool. When drumming groups who are struggling for coherence and meditation are taken over by angry, mindless bashers, the whole world suffers.

In jazz improvization, there are rules that the band must follow. One primary rule is that the melody must be repeated at the end of the song. After all the soloing and hot licks, the original melody must be played coherently, just as at the beginning of the song. Why is that? It is a reentry into our sphere of being from that other place outside our world where only the great players can take us. It is a necessary reentry that attempts to make sense out of the fantastic journey on which the players have taken the audience. It is essential to the well being of the audience and the players that the tune be concluded in a coherent manner. If this doesn't happen, then the psyche of the listener and the player is fractured and confused. That is no way to step out into the street after a hot session. The same thing is very important in a drumming group.

The habit for many drumming groups is to drum up to a high degree of excitement, then stop. It's a dramatic and fun way to end. Sometimes, this can be damaging. It can inadvertently create an angry state of mind if our soul is trying to use the drumming as a way to commune with higher sources of energy. When we generate a higher level of energy, the soul is taken to a higher place of communion. When the journey is nearing the end, it is imperative that the drummers bring back the drumbeat to some semblance of the original energy level so that the soul can journey back to its body. Restating the original melody calls the spirit back into the body in a gentle way. Some kind of symbolic restating of the original idea that started the whole journey is a satisfying way to end a drumming group. Without this conclusion, a piece of our soul can be left flailing around in a confused universe with no solid resolution. Our conscious mind and our soul needs to have a good ending to the trip. This is body and soul integration.

That may be one reason there are a lot of angry drummers; they don't go back to "the head" and close the tune properly. This is akin to a schizophrenic break. I try to always bring the drumming group back down to this vibrational level in a gradual and peaceful way so as not to leave the participants in a psychotic state. Life leaves us in psychotic states all the time. Drumming is a way to regain the integration that we are so hungry for. Just remember to bring it back down after you have gone "out there" and everyone will be happy and peaceful. If you stop when everyone is still out there, then you will have problems right away—possibly big problems.

Some drumming groups are attracting the attention of the local police. The police have to watch out for angry energy. They are trained to deal with it. When a drumming group is uncaring as to its effect on the community, then the police are called in to remind them that they are part of the community, and there are responsibilities that must be respected. When the police sense anger, they react. When the police sense a peaceful situation, they tend to relax somewhat.

We have a Cherokee friend who is a police officer. He sings sacred Indian songs at the Powwows. He can be a formidable opponent, but essentially he is an honorable and gentle man who seeks peace with himself and the world. He plays a drum for that sense of peace, yet he is a man who daily must deal

The greatest and quietest creative healing has worked through the drum.

with violence and anger. He has a vocabulary in both worlds. Most of us don't have a vocabulary for our anger. It is either there at full boil or it is tucked away and repressed, waiting to explode at the next inappropriate moment. The drum can give us a vocabulary for our anger. It is a way to understand force and power in a controlled, elegant manner. Drumming gives us words for our state of anger as well as our state of grace. When we have the words to articulate our anger, then the anger is not so overpowering. There is a way out.

We can feel the power through the drum and not succumb to the excess that a violent society is selling. The drum can bring the world through times of struggle, into a commonality of purpose and healing where understanding can be as pervasive as the air we breath. The drum has done this for me. I have forgiven and I have grown through this simple, yet powerful tool. I don't have any special gift. I came to this process because I needed something. I have seen it save other people's lives in different ways. There is joy in the playing and the dancing and the feeling, and it doesn't take any special knowledge or training. The happiness is almost immediate, and the mystery remains, no matter how much learning one does.

I have seen many people who are physically hurt come to the drum as a way to heal, or at least to free themselves from the pain for at least a little while. This is not me doing this to them. These are people who have never drummed before, making an effort to help themselves. They overcome physical handicaps, emotional turmoil, psychological trauma, and social conditioning to arrive at a place of harmony and balance where tapping your hand on a drumhead is as easy as smiling.

If I can do it, anyone can do it.

Some people are so in love with drumming that they hurt themselves. They speak of sore elbows and sprained wrists. This is sometimes a byproduct of a certain psychological approach to whatever these people are doing in their lives. They bear down so hard that they hurt themselves. The compulsiveness that they bring to anything they do will show up in the drumming too. So I recommend to the people who are feeling injured that they play much softer, with quick gentleness instead of intensity.

The intensity is a holdover from the day-to-day struggle in our modern society. The drum should be a way to free ourselves from the rat race, not wound ourselves anymore than we already have been. The drum is a sensitive instrument. Hitting it just enough to get the tone vibrating in the drum is what is needed. Hitting the drum too hard makes a brittle sound that is irritating. Hitting it too hard will hurt you. I am all for getting it on and hitting hard, but the way to hit the drum can be very mystical. This way it is a "non-hit." The note springs up from the vibrating drumhead without much skin on skin effort at all. I enjoy this kind of drumming because I don't have to work hard. It is easier to play lightly, plus I have more stamina for the long drumming events. The subtlety of lower volume adds a great deal of magical energy that loud drumming will overpower.

When the players speak of injuries, I see that their compulsive attitudes are many times creating the injuries. The drum articulates it. By playing softer, a new way of looking at the world unfolds for some people. They realize that they don't have to fight. They come to realize that the universe is a supportive friend rather than an adversary. Playing softly is also a way to play in an apartment or house where other people might not be willing to be pummeled into submission by loud drumming. I have seen neighbors come around to allowing someone to play the drum if it is done in a soft, relaxing manner. This can be a soothing balm for a worried mind if it is done without the angst and intensity that so many people assume is the only way to play a drum.

Big Sur, 1989. After having given up on the music business I only played in private moments of solitude. A drummer had set up on the cliffs overlooking the Pacific Ocean—I stopped and talked. My long stretch of thirst ended when I decided to play with this total stranger. There was no stage, no loudspeakers, no lights, no managers, no agents, no audience. Only the great Mother Ocean. I began to heal and share the rhythms of nature, and I started to find my way back to the path that was right for me.

29

LESSONS

There are many different ways to learn to play the drum. The drum is not a musical instrument in this particular process so you don't have to be afraid of making a mistake. The point in this type of drumming is to let the feel carry you.

Many times, I see people who really need to learn lessons. It is a comfort to them. The tendency is to learn with their intellect, and then to play from their intellect, but the body plays the drum. The brain just learns.

I have looked for ways to teach rhythm theory to people so they get it directly into their bodies with no filtering through their brain. When people learn this way they don't think they are learning, because the sensation of playing gets easy very quickly. There is no anxiety involved.

Here is an interesting way to understand rhythm: subtracting notes. Set up a pattern of even back and forth notes, using both hands equally. We'll call this: "Pa Ta Pa Ta."

"Pa Ta Pa Ta Pa Ta Pa Ta Pa Ta Pa Ta Pa Ta Pa Ta Pa Ta."

Now remember this should be a relaxed tempo. Not too fast. It will get tricky if you speed up. Take a big breath and settle in at a "walking tempo," as opposed to a jogging tempo.

Now hit the drum five times: "Pa Ta Pa Ta Pa."

Leave a pause or a "breath," then hit the same five notes again.

After another short breath, again hit the five notes.

Keep doing five notes, then a pause, until it settles into a comfortable pattern. Now relax your breathing and let it fall back into its own tempo.

Next take out the third note, leave a little space just where the third note would be, and keep the rest of the pattern going. It is fewer notes, but has a better feel. Alternate back and forth between playing the five notes steady, then playing the same pattern without the third note. This starts to become a longer phrase. This sort of becomes a rumba.

On the next page is a visual representation of some of these rhythms. I have tried to simplify the notation so as to make it a more direct experience.

If you can't make this work, that's a good sign. That means you might just be able to hear it and get it without having to do all this thinking.

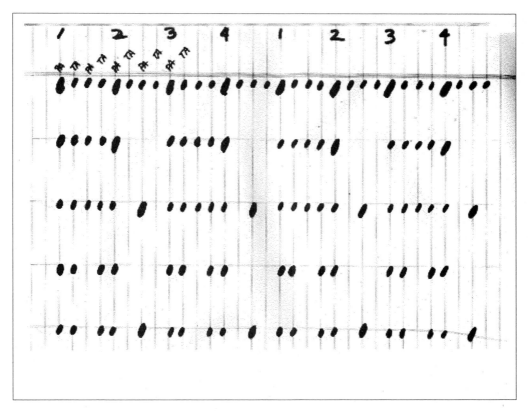

"Pa Ta Pa Ta."

CONCLUSION

I wish to thank all of the people who have shown me the true magic in the drum, the students who have shared their journey with me. I have witnessed what they received from this ancient friend. Sometimes I don't feel like having a drumming workshop, but as soon as I start to drum the journey becomes compelling for me. The people who come and ask to play and learn and share are my teachers, and I'm grateful for the opportunity to share something so profound with so many interesting people.

Of course, the only reason this kind of thing works is because it's fun. There is a simple joyous truth that in each of our lives there is a perfectly correct place for celebrating life and giving thanks.

I have been a drummer my whole life, but that has really just been the vehicle for me to explore who I am and how I feel and heal. People eager to embark on a journey using the drum can find their way very easily. The support seems to be everywhere now. I had almost given up on finding a way to drum and to be true to some sort of inner voice that told me how to use the drum as a gift for people; not just for making money.

I have always known that there is a powerful spirit ready to emerge as soon as the drum begins, but until now drumming meant being locked into a dreary existence playing Top 40 songs or easy listening jazz that lacked any spiritual sustenance. I refused to do that. For a time I gave up what I loved because there was no place where the magic was allowed to come through. I have come to realize that the magic is everywhere and the drum can articulate the magic at any time and any place with profound results. This can be called a sacred energy in any language and in any religious doctrine you choose. The spirit of the Divine can be called into the humble recipient. I am excited that our culture is now discovering this rhythmic source of inspiration. There are, no doubt, a lot of people who want to make money from this new fad, but that won't change the real phenomenon of magical drumming. For some it has never been a fad. It's not a fad for me. I have made and lost money and other things too with the drum—such as friendship and partners. One of the greatest gifts in the drum is that it enables us to share our heart's energy with other people. In creating music, the players become each other and weave the tune together. The mingling of spirits is an unnameable mystery that is richer than any gold records on a wall.

I am grateful that I learned the drum as an instrument. It gave me the opportunity to learn greater things about soul and magic and also provided a musical language that describes some of these mysteries. The songwriters that I have worked with have used music to tell their tales and I have supported their songs with my drumming. I have kept my voice out of the way so as not to interfere with their stories. This book has been a way for me to explain and describe and encourage in words what I have always done with the drum. Words are great, but I'd rather be drumming.

Everyone has access to this joy. It takes a small amount of effort and a little bit of courage to hit the drum, but after the first note almost everybody is willing to continue the beat. That is the beat of life and love. The energy that comes through is a nurturing, positive force that heals, enlightens, and blesses the participants.

Allowing yourself to feel this creative healing energy flow through you is to let the Goddess dance in yourself. Then we can share it with the world.

Let the drumming continue, and *let the Goddess dance.*

photo by Charles Turkington

Buddy Helm leads a workshop at Seasons. Behind him is his partner, Cathleen Javier.

REACH FOR THE MOON

Llewellyn publishes hundreds of books on your favorite subjects! To get these exciting books, including the ones on the following pages, check your local bookstore or order them directly from Llewellyn.

Order by Phone

- Call toll-free within the U.S. and Canada, 1-800-THE MOON
- In Minnesota, call (651) 291-1970
- We accept VISA, MasterCard, and American Express

ORDER BY MAIL

- Send the full price of your order (MN residents add 7% sales tax) in U.S. funds, plus postage & handling to:

  Llewellyn Worldwide
  P.O. Box 64383, Dept. K432-4
  St. Paul, MN 55164–0383, U.S.A.

POSTAGE & HANDLING

(For the U.S., Canada, and Mexico)

- $4.00 for orders $15.00 and under
- $5.00 for orders over $15.00
- No charge for orders over $100.00

We ship UPS in the continental United States. We ship standard mail to P.O. boxes. Orders shipped to Alaska, Hawaii, The Virgin Islands, and Puerto Rico are sent first-class mail. Orders shipped to Canada and Mexico are sent surface mail.

International orders: Airmail—add freight equal to price of each book to the total price of order, plus $5.00 for each non-book item (audio tapes, etc.).
Surface mail—Add $1.00 per item.

Allow 2 weeks for delivery on all orders.
Postage and handling rates subject to change.

DISCOUNTS

We offer a 20% discount to group leaders or agents. You must order a minimum of 5 copies of the same book to get our special quantity price.

FREE CATALOG

Get a free copy of our color catalog, *New Worlds of Mind and Spirit*. Subscribe for just $10.00 in the United States and Canada ($30.00 overseas, airmail). Many bookstores carry *New Worlds*—ask for it!

Visit our website at www.llewellyn.com for more information.

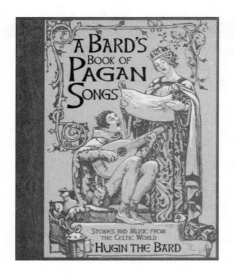

A BARD'S BOOK OF PAGAN SONGS

Stories and Music from the Celtic World

Now with music CD inside!

Hugin the Bard

1-56718-658-0
272 pp., 8¼ x 10 $19.95

Enchant the ears and imaginations of all who hear you play the fifty original songs in this book. Plus, you can now hear Hugin the Bard perform selections from the book on the CD that has just been added!

Everything you need to perform the songs is provided: complete lyrics, chord charts, and lead sheets with the key signature, chords, and melody lines. Each song is accompanied by a story, tale, or bit of Pagan lore, all set down in Hugin's own calligraphy.

The new CD features Hugin's enthusiastic rendition of "Bardic Tales from the Mabinogion." The Mabinogion is a collection of ancient Welsh tales, put down in the old Welsh language in the sixth century. Hugin brings them to life with song, guitar, and storytelling in the 60-minute CD.

- Celebrate the Goddess, magic, love, and adventure through songs, chants, and stories
- Immerse yourself in the beautiful tales from the Mabinogion
- Journey through the Wheel of the Year with eleven songs that honor the Sabbats
- Raise energy for your Circles, feasts, and gatherings with Hugin's unique chants and invocations
- Make your rituals more rewarding and fun

Jeraldine Saunders. Her name is synonymous with bringing romance to the high seas. She single-handedly revived the cruise industry with her book "The Love Boats" which became a household phrase throughout the world and the inspiration for the popular "Love Boat" television series. Now Llewellyn is proud to present this two-book set featuring *Love Boats,* the real-life story of the creator of the TV series, plus *Love Signs,* Jeraldine Saunders' manual of romantic and sexual compatibility.

Love Boats: Above and Below Decks with Jeraldine Saunders is offered in this special 2-volume Collector's Edition. It's an expanded edition of the original, full of black and white photographs, plus a 16-page color section, and true tales of love and hate, sex and silliness, greed and generosity, beauties and beasts, Bali Hai and Shangri-La.

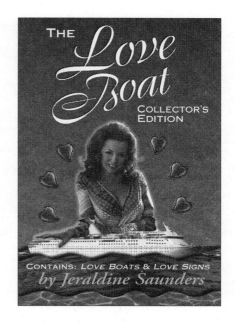

THE LOVE BOAT COLLECTOR'S EDITION

Includes the books *Love Boats* AND *Love Signs*

Jeraldine Saunders

Either book available singly:

Love Boats 1-56718-607-6 $12.95

Love Signs 1-56718-618-1 $12.95

1-56718-614-9

Two-book set

Love Boats: 336 pp., 6 x 9, + 16-pg. color photo insert

Love Signs: 320 pp., 6 x 9

$24.95

The compact disk accompanying this book

Let the Goddess Dance
by
Russell S. Buddy Helm

is a production of Buddy Helm Music BMI. All songs written by Russell S. Buddy Helm. All music performed by Russell S. Buddy Helm.

For bookings, workshops, and lessons, contact:
website: buddyhelm.com   email: buddyrsh@ix.netcom.com

Special thanks to Steve Sanzo at Bungalow Productions, Eagle Rock, California, for immaculate production of the Drum Meditations.

Thank you to Gregory, a realized master of sound recording, for your patience and generosity in helping me hear.

———

"Fertile Delta" drum meditation is inspired by the place where the land meets the water. It is the place of rich, fecund possibilities, specifically where the Nile meets the Mediterranean, but there is a fertile Delta everywhere.

"Salome" is the dance of the seven veils. The illusions drop away with the veils, sensual enlightenment through the power of the rhythm.

"Power Tools." The drum is a power tool. Careful!

"Mountain Thunder." The place where dark energy resides. The place of creation. Movement under our feet. Movement in our ears. Movement in our bodies and souls.

"Nightpath." Walking down a mysterious jungle path that is both exciting and beautiful.

"Drum Dance." Dance to heal, based on a great chiropractic breakthrough of my own healing.

"Spirits Around You." A result of the Psychic readings in Clearwater with Hoyt Robinette where I met my Spirit Guardians and my relatives who are supporting me in the drumming healing workshops. Chief Many Horns said that it was important work because it brought people up to a higher level. He and Sister Mary Lucretia are two of my Spirit Guardians, along with my Grandmother Lily Helm, my father Russell, and his brother Roy Helm

"Let the Goddess Dance." I felt the need to find songs which we can use to celebrate a new birth of consciousness.

Instrumentation: Egyptian Dombeq, Moroccan clay derbouga, claves, finger cymbals, bell tree, Congas, Tibetan cymbals, Zildjian cymbals, Yamaha sg35 keyboard, Gretch drums. Oaxacan Jaguar flute, Ghana Djembe and Ashiko, African ago-go bells, Fender and Gibson guitars.